Deliverance
and
Spiritual Body
Mapping

CAROLYN STEIDLEY

BALBOA.
PRESS
A DIVISION OF HAY HOUSE

Balboa Press books may be ordered through booksellers or by contacting:

Balboa Press
A Division of Hay House
1663 Liberty Drive
Bloomington, IN 47403
www.balboapress.com
1 (877) 407-4847

Because of the dynamic nature of the Internet, any web addresses or links contained in this book may have changed since publication and may no longer be valid. The views expressed in this work are solely those of the author and do not necessarily reflect the views of the publisher, and the publisher hereby disclaims any responsibility for them.

The author of this book does not dispense medical advice or prescribe the use of any technique as a form of treatment for physical, emotional, or medical problems without the advice of a physician, either directly or indirectly. The intent of the author is only to offer information of a general nature to help you in your quest for emotional and spiritual well-being. In the event you use any of the information in this book for yourself, which is your constitutional right, the author and the publisher assume no responsibility for your actions.

Any people depicted in stock imagery provided by Thinkstock are models, and such images are being used for illustrative purposes only.
Certain stock imagery © Thinkstock.

Print information available on the last page.

ISBN: 978-1-5043-5981-8 (sc)
ISBN: 978-1-5043-5982-5 (hc)
ISBN: 978-1-5043-6012-8 (e)

Library of Congress Control Number: 2016909496

Balboa Press rev. date: 06/08/2016

TABLE OF CONTENTS

DEDICATION

I would like to express my profound grateful appreciation to the people who made this book possible, first and foremost, my husband Robert for driving to the desert with me to fast and pray for seven days while the Lord downloaded what turned out to be two books, and to my mother, Janice Simpson Linder, who assisted me in every aspect of writing and publishing the book; my sister, Melissa McCrery, for assisting in the last push of writing the manuscript; my mentors, Coy and Donna Huffman, for saying, "You can ride this horse"; Melody Morrison, for being brave enough to ride this horse with me; Kirby Molen, for his encouragement and direction; Dude Overton, for her gentle prodding to complete the task and for all the encouragement; and Sandy Roller, for being my friend and side-kick.

Lastly, I would like to thank all of the people who through the years have asked for this book to be written.

God Bless you!

FOREWORD

As a world champion All- Around Cowgirl, multiple- term president, and ministry co-founder of the National Christian Barrel Racing Association, and co-pastor of Cowboy Country Church Outreach Ministry, I would inevitably, cross paths with Carolyn. She is a trainer of National Reined Cow Horses, founder of the Glory Riders West Coast Division, and pastor of Manger Ministries. The first time we met, in an arena, she captured my attention from "hello".

We have in common the unique gift of "mapping" our way through the "wilderness" and *many times* out of trouble. Carolyn has used this gift, love for others, and her knowledge of how to maneuver out of the traps of the enemy in her passionate teaching. Using the Sword of the Spirit like a surgeon uses a scalpel, she is able to deliver and set free those held in bondage.

In this book, she blazes a trail through this ground-breaking teaching of how the body harbors our spiritual emotions. It is a must read for those who have found themselves in the chains of inequity, the depths of depression, or the ravages of rejection. As I read this book, I was amazed at how easy the instructions are to understand. Yes, anyone can "get it." Her teachings line up with scripture and are delightfully full of her humorous stories as she navigates toward introducing Spiritual Body Mapping.

This scripture has more meaning than ever before:

> As ye go, preach, saying the Kingdom of heaven is
> at hand, heal the sick, cleanse the lepers, raise the

dead, cast out devils; freely ye have received, freely give." (Matt. 10:7-8, KJV)

Cowgirl to cowgirl: "Carolyn, thanks for the guided tour. It has helped me find 'TRUE NORTH' regarding my personal release from dead-end roads that I was on. I am now able to show others there is a way out ..."

—Rev. Dude Overton, co-pastor of Cowboy Country Church Outreach Ministry, co-founder and past president of NCBRA, three-time world champion All-Around Cowgirl (NSPRA)

DISCLAIMER

The contents of this book are for personal knowledge only. They are not intended to conflict with the advice of doctors or professional counselors. The information within the pages of this book is not intended to conflict with church doctrines or practices.

I am not responsible for any person's disease, mental or spiritual health, or their healing.

I am not a professional. I am sharing the Word of God according to Mark 16:15.

INTRODUCTION

I was a twenty-one-year-old cocktail waitress. My husband was a bartender. We lived in a small apartment in town. At the time, we were both working part-time while attending college. I cannot explain it, but I began to feel compelled to start attending a large charismatic church in our area. As I began to attend, strange things started to happen around the apartment. I would put something down only to return a while later, and it would be gone. I would walk past the closet, and the clothes would be swinging inside. I would yell at my husband, "Come here *quick!*" And sure enough, by the time he would get there, the clothes would be still again. I began to think something was psychologically wrong with me.

One fall afternoon, I was in the living room of our small apartment talking to my aunt on the phone. She was trying to encourage me to come to the revival her Pentecostal church was having that night. I laughed and told her that I had not picked up my Bible in a very long time. She said, "Carolyn, just open it."

I replied, "No, Aunt Dell, I have a wall between the Bible and me."

She became persistent. "Carolyn! You get your Bible right now!"

I reluctantly got out of the armchair and went to the bedroom, found the Bible, and walked back into the living room, all the while talking with Aunt Dell on the phone. I sat back down in the armchair and opened the book. Immediately, I felt a presence in the room, and it was angry. My breath caught in my throat, and I gasped into the phone, "Aunt Dell, I am not alone!"

"What is wrong, Carolyn?" I tried to explain what was happening in the room. The more I talked, the more ominous the presence became, and I became very fearful and told my aunt I was scared. She asked me where I felt safe in the apartment. I told her in the kitchen. She instructed me to go there; I obeyed. We continued our conversation with me standing fearfully in the kitchen, wanting nothing better than to tuck my tail and run for all I was worth.

Aunt Dell encouraged me to come to my grandmother's house where she was visiting. Nanny and Papa were Pentecostal preachers and had been missionaries in Mexico and went on to build a church there. I told her I would come immediately. I arrived at Nanny's house a bit flustered. Aunt Dell, Nanny and I talked for a while, and in the end, they talked me into going to church with them that night. I remember telling them I did not have on the "right" clothes. I was wearing blue jeans, and the church they attended did not like women to wear pants to church. "No problem!" Aunt Dell quickly replied. "You can wear one of Nanny's dresses!" Now here I am, a twenty-one-year-old cocktail waitress getting into her Nanny's dress that looked like it was from the 1950s. I could feel the flush in my cheeks as I looked at myself in the mirror. Since it was wintertime, I borrowed one of her dress coats as well. *Oh boy*, I thought. *Here we go.*

I remember arriving at the church where the revival was taking place. Aunt Dell and Nanny were so happy I was with them. As for me, I tried to sit against a wall, the farthest away from the front that I could find. The elder women would have none of that, though. They compromised with me and sat me in the middle. I sat through the sermon with Nanny's coat tightly wrapped around me and watched the clock. I wondered how long that long-winded preacher was going to talk.

At the end of the service, he gave an altar call. Several people went to the altar and stood in a line—I was not one of them. Then, that preacher did the most incredible thing. He called the whole church up to the front. I thought, *Great, now what?*

I obediently, yet reluctantly, marched up to the altar and stood in the line with everyone else. The preacher started praying at one end. As he prayed, different people would fall to the floor under the power of the Holy Spirit. This was not new to me, because I had grown up under my papa's teachings. Papa had been a pastor of a church where signs and wonders were quite common. It was not until later that, as a teenager, I had strayed from the Lord.

As the pastor continued down the line, I watched him warily. I could feel myself getting ready to bolt. He reached the person next to me, and I was gone. I ran for my chair and buried my head in my hands. How my grandmother got there so fast, I will never know.

The next thing I heard was "What's wrong, girl?"

"Nanny, I have never been afraid of a Pentecostal preacher before," I sobbed. She took hold of me by the ear and back up to the altar we went. I stood before that preacher like a bull looking at a new gate. I asked Nanny, "Do I have to tell him what is going on in my apartment?"

"No! Let me tell *you* what is going on!" the preacher boomed. "As you sat back there during this service, there was a huge chain wrapped around your body and neck; in the links of the chain was a snake. And, as you sat there, it was pulling tighter and tighter. Young lady, had you left here tonight, you would not have made it." As he spoke, I could feel my body begin to shake violently; I was having a hard time standing up. He went on to say, "I am going to pray for you, and when I do you will feel the power of the Holy Ghost as you have never felt Him before!" The pastor started to walk toward me, and as he did, I was thrown hard to the floor. This was not the work of the Lord; it was an evil spirit trying to get away from that man of God.

He prayed and continued to pray until I finally felt relief. The pastor then gave me a prayer cloth to take to my apartment. My apartment was on the second floor of the building. As I walked up those stairs that night with the prayer cloth in my hand, I could sense fear on the other side of the door. I put the key in the lock and opened the door. And sure enough, the "thing" was gone!

That day marked a turning point in my life. A few weeks later, I met a very godly woman by the name of Gloria Strouse. She and her husband Wes were the directors of Maranatha House. Mutual friends had given me her phone number. Gloria operated in the deliverance ministry. I called her and invited her over to my apartment to learn more about this whole "deliverance" thing.

I remember answering the door on the day of our first meeting. I have to chuckle, because after our telephone conversation, I'd been expecting a powerhouse of a woman. In my mind, she had to be ten feet tall and bullet proof. Instead, I opened the door and looked right over the top of her head. However, I came to find out that dynamite can come in small packages.

We sat on the sofa and got acquainted. She then turned the subject as to why she was there—to spiritually clean out the apartment. She explained how to clean a house, and then she casually informed me that I, too, had demonic activity within me. I was stunned.

"What? What do you mean?" I asked.

She began to teach me how the spirits operated, and I started to see their influence in my life. I said, "Let's get them out! Right now!"

She smiled and said, "Oh no, I never work alone. We will have to set up an appointment for a couple of weeks from now."

"You've got to be kidding! You inform me I have demons, and you are going to leave me here with them?" I gasped.

Again, she smiled. "Oh, they aren't going anywhere. We will evict them soon."

I am here to tell you, that was the longest two weeks of my life, waiting for my deliverance appointment. Unbeknownst to me, that meeting with Gloria was the start of my life in the work of the Lord.

Two weeks later, I met her for my appointment. That was when I met Dick and Violet Van Devere. They were the most compassionate couple I had ever met. They oozed love and mercy. We sat in their living room and visited, and I felt myself becoming agitated and restless. I tried to hide it from the three of them, but I fidgeted on the sofa. Soon, they stood up and announced that it was time to begin. I remember the blood pounding in my ears and the churning of my stomach. *What is wrong with me?*

They placed me in a chair while Gloria sat across from me in another chair and led me in a renunciation and forgiveness prayer. As we were reciting this prayer, I could feel what seemed like bands around me and air bubbles moving in my abdomen, legs, and arms. My thoughts became frantic: *This is crazy. I need to get out of here. Run!* But my legs would not work.

After we had finished the prayer, they began to call out various names of spirits. Oh wow—I could hear in my head voices talking back and forth, calling the ministers dirty names and screaming. I could feel their rage at having to leave their "house." They were possessive over me and had no intention of coming out. I became somewhat detached, like I was merely watching all this play out. As the ministers continued, I could feel the spirits go from rage to fear. They started to try to "make deals" with the ministers so they could stay. They began to "tell on" each other. There was absolutely no loyalty among them. In my head was pure chaos.

I remember at one point Mrs. Van Devere placing a Bible between my back and the chair. Oh my gosh—my body immediately turned into Jell-O—without any bones. I slid to the floor, resisting the touch of the Word of God, groaning out loud. After several hours of intense, combative spiritual warfare, I was set free. Two things stand out to me about that event.

1. It was the first time my mind was quiet; previously, my mind had always been working;
2. My whole body felt like a cast had been taken off of it. I felt like I had lost thirty pounds. I wanted to float.

In the weeks that followed, I could feel love like never before, and the colors around me seemed to be brighter. Most of all, there were no walls anymore between the Bible and me. Life was good.

The Lord formed a spiritual bond between Gloria and myself. She took this strong-willed young woman under her wing and began to teach me, using love, compassion, and understanding. She had the patience of Job! I continued to work with Gloria over the years to develop my spiritual gifts. I became her armor bearer, just as Elisha became Elijah's armor bearer. I trained with her and the Van Deveres, taking classes on deliverance, studying Derek Prince's teaching on deliverance as well as others. The studying and on-the-job training was intense. At the same time, I was attending a Bible college. It was exciting to see the Glory of God manifested!

I praise God that He would walk right into a bar and pull this girl out. I have much to be thankful for: He truly is my Redeemer. I am grateful that He gave me such outstanding teachers in the deliverance ministry. They were sold out to their calling; they gave up so much, according to the world's standards, to live the life they chose, that of the Kingdom of God. They have all since gone home to be with the Lord, but their ministry continues through the people they trained.

I have to laugh when I recall the first time I was asked to do a deliverance myself without one of my teachers. I received a phone call at about ten one night. It was my cousin's husband. He said that

Denise, my cousin, was at work at the hospital that night and every time she would talk to someone about the Lord she would double over in pain. The pain was intense, and she needed my help. *What? My help?* "Okay," I said, "come over."

I hung up the phone. *What am I going to do?* I immediately went into the bedroom and told my husband, "I am not sure, but I don't think you should be sleeping while we do a deliverance." Now, you have to understand, my husband was still bartending and had not accepted Jesus as his Savior yet. To be honest, this deliverance stuff freaked him out.

I heard the knock on the door, and I opened it to see Jeff supporting a slouched-over Denise. *Lord, what do I do?* I sat her in a chair and looked at Jeff. "Jeff, you are going to have to help me."

"No problem," came his answer. We began with the renunciation and forgiveness prayer, which she repeated. I then started to call out different names of spirits as the Lord gave me names through the gift of discernment and word of knowledge. Denise began to heave; I grabbed a towel.

I looked over at my husband to see him sitting in a chair across the room reading the Bible. I looked closer, and the Bible was upside down. Fear had froze him to the chair. He was terrified. I was busy, though, and could not worry about it at that moment. I continued working on Denise. She vomited into the towel. I asked her, "What did you have for dinner?"

"Fish, why?" she answered.

"Because what I am looking at is not fish." What I held in the towel looked like a piece of beef liver. As soon as she threw it up, she was out of pain.

In the weeks that followed, Denise was healed of a hernia. We learned that deliverance and healing go hand in hand. Deliverance gets rid of the entity that causes problems in the body. Once it is cast out, then healing can begin. After this event with Jeff and Denise, the family started to understand that I had not fallen into a "cult thing." They realized there was a "God thing" going on instead.

One day, I received a phone call from a couple from the church I attended. They were having problems and wanted to talk to me. I had already discerned that this couple was dealing with demonic activity but had not had the opportunity to minister to them. The husband wanted to know when I could come to their house. I told him I would need to get back to him and called my mother for help. Mom was very hesitant at the thought of actually getting involved in a deliverance. So she made me promise that I would not do a deliverance while she was there, that we would just go to counsel the couple. I agreed and called the couple back to set up an appointment.

A few days later, Mom and I pulled up to the couple's house. It was an older small home, perfect for a new couple starting out. We sat in the living room and began to talk. They were having marital problems. But as we continued to talk, the demons in the husband began to manifest. I have learned that the children of the Lord, who know their authority in Christ, walk in an authority that the adversary recognizes and hates. Demons will manifest when the anointing is present.

So here we were, the couple seated in two chairs across from Mom and me. As the demons in the man became more prominent, the man's ears ran up the side of his head and stood out. The man's countenance changed and became contorted. He looked like something out of a science fiction movie. In everyday life, it was unexplainable. I looked over at Mom, knowing I had promised not to do a deliverance. She looked startled and later told me she saw an angel standing behind the man and the angel told her it was okay.

That was the beginning of Mom and I becoming a team in deliverance. She has since penned a book entitled *Are you Ready for War?*

Mom and I have worked for many years in this type of ministry. The deliverance ministry is something I did not seek. It is terribly exhausting and, to say the least, dirty. But when confronted with a person who needs a deliverance, I will not back down.

It is important to know the difference between deliverance and exorcism. Francis MacNutt puts it this way: "An exorcism is a prayer to deliver someone who is possessed, whereas a deliverance is a prayer to deliver someone who possesses or is oppressed by an evil spirit."[1] I have been involved in both types of ministry.

Through the years, the Holy Spirit began to show me ways that would expedite the deliverance process. Please understand there are no formulas with the Lord. He is sovereign and will do things as He sees fit. So understand that in the following chapter, I am not giving you a formula. I am giving you something to add to your repertoire in diagnosing, freeing, and releasing a person who is in need of an inner healing and/or deliverance.

PART I

IDENTIFYING AND EXPOSING THE ENEMY'S ACCESS TO OUR BODY

CHAPTER 1

BEFORE WE BEGIN

Before we begin, I need to make something very clear: Deliverance is not an event; it is a process. Deliverance is the casting out or away of demons and other dark forces. However, after the demon has vacated, the individual's toxic thinking and bad habits must be addressed. It is important to enroll the person in a discipleship program following their session.

When working in deliverance, be prepared to work outside the box but always in alignment with the Bible. In this type of ministry, you will see a lot of things that will blow your mind. Always remember that none of what the enemy does is a surprise to the Lord. He will guide and lead you to defeat your adversary. After all, your victory over the enemy is your inheritance, according to Isaiah 54:16-17. The Lord created the waster to destroy; He went on to state that no weapon formed against the believer will prosper. The Lord is on your side when dealing with the enemy.

Several years ago, I became quite upset after losing two mentors to cancer; one was my teacher in ministry, and the other was my mentor in training horses.

One day, I was angrily pacing in my living room, telling the Lord what I thought about this whole matter. (I do not recommend taking this attitude toward the Lord. I was young and immature.)

I told the Lord, "I am tired of being a pawn on a chessboard stuck between two kings—a black king and a white king!"

I heard the Lord speak quite audibly in the room; I have only heard Him talk to me like this once. "Yes, I put you there. But I made you the queen to go anywhere you want to go."

There was a pause. Then He said, "And it is the ultimate slap in my enemy's face that he is subject to a mere mortal."

I was stunned. I had not thought about things like that. The Lord told me, "I gave you the authority to take the enemy out, now do it!"

There are a few things to consider before delving into doing a deliverance. First, make sure that the person needs one. Ask the Holy Spirit, "Does this person need a deliverance?" Your discernment should tell you, but if you are not sure, wait. One can do a lot of damage when one attempts a so-called deliverance on an individual who needs psychological help or an inner healing instead.

Second, be sure that you understand the difference between the soul realm and the spiritual realm. I find this is a real problem in ministry. I want to state the obvious: Not everything is a spirit. Sometimes the person needs inner healing or physical healing. Be open to working with doctors. While they work on the mental or physical body, you address the spiritual issues.

It is imperative that you hear from the Lord on what the person needs: healing, deliverance, or a counselor. Deliverance and healing go hand in hand; for that matter, so does deliverance and counseling. I have lost count of how many times a person will be delivered from an evil spirit and is physically healed in the same session.

Deliverance and healing are two separate issues. A demon can cause damage to a person's body. After the demon has been cast out, the damage may remain, at which point healing needs to take place.

As a matter of fact, at this time, we have thirty-four people delivered and healed from cancer.

Do I Speak Aloud to a Demon?

People have asked me, "Do I have to speak out loud to a demon?" The answer is no.

Now, I know that will go against many individuals' theology. I too was raised to believe that a demon cannot hear your thoughts. Then I encountered a situation that challenged me. A family member was in the ICU and dying; I was asked to come. The ICU room was swarming with doctors and nurses as they frantically worked to save the person.

I silently rebuked the spirit of death and told it to leave as I stood in the doorway. I then left and sat down in the waiting room. Within an hour, a doctor came out to tell everyone that our family member in the ICU was going to be all right.

Later, I asked the Lord about that situation, as it went against everything I thought I understood about spirits not being able to read my thoughts. His answer to me was, "They can hear your spirit." That made sense, of course.

Who Should Not Get Involved

I believe there are those who should not get involved in deliverance. One should first be baptized in the Holy Spirit. I would hate to attempt a session without the Holy Spirit.

In Francis MacNutt's book *Healing*, he points out three different personality types that should not get involved in ministering in deliverance.

The first are those who are hyper-sensitive to attacks in the spirit realm. They are vulnerable and, therefore, open to the enemy. The second personality would be a person who is "too aggressive." This person enjoys the fight way too much. Hatred for the enemy should not be the motive for deliverance. Love and compassion for the individual who is the victim should be the motivation. We must always work out of God's fruit of the Spirit. The third would be a person who is motivated by power.[1]

Of course, it can be a rush when the demons fight and lose. If you are not careful to stay humble, your ego can be a stumbling block. The most powerful position there is in the kingdom of God is humility. There is spiritual vision and clarity of sight from that position.

In this type of ministry, people will develop an area of specialty. Let me explain: It seems the Lord will bring a set type of deliverance to these ministers. An example would be what we could call team A; the Lord will lead people who battle depression to this team. This team becomes proficient in dealing with these types of spirits. To team B, the Lord may bring people who want to be set free from the occult; team B would become proficient in these types of spirits, and so on.

The problem I see is that sometimes these ministers, when they hit a block and can't seem to progress, may hesitate to send someone to a different healing/deliverance team.

On the flip side, I have seen a group that has sent an individual to another healing ministry, and the second team will look down on the first team, not realizing that a particular spirit is not the first team's forte.

It all boils down to pride. Pride has no place in a believer's life, let alone a ministry team.

No Formulas with God

Please do not get caught up in the idea that there is only one way to minister in inner healing and/or deliverance. I believe in studying the different aspects of ministry, such as sozo and terraforming, which are both different styles of inner healing. As well as traditional deliverance, which is speaking directly to the enemy and casting him out or away from an individual, much the same way Jesus did in the New Testament. Finally, there is spiritual body mapping, which I will explain more later in this book. By studying the different styles you can take what works for yourself and develop your own style.

Allow the Holy Spirit to direct you. Take what you learn and put the information in your quiver so you have it when you need it. The more you educate yourself, the more empowered you will be and the more versatile your work for the Lord.

It is important to be skilled in this ministry, as there are principles we need to know and understand in the kingdom of God. Also, consider that people are individuals, and no two are alike. There are no formulas. God is sovereign and will do things according to His will. The more trained we are, the more prepared we will be when confronted with a new situation and when working with different personality types.

I began to have a clearer understanding when I was asked to teach a deliverance class in Arizona. After the class, many of the students requested a session. I could see the longing to walk with the Lord in the manner I had described possible.

Throughout the two-day meeting, we were able to deliver seventeen people, and some of them received either a physical or inner healing as well. The Lord supernaturally developed teams, and as one person got delivered, she or he would get out of their chair and begin helping the next person get delivered. It was the most amazing and humbling thing I've ever seen. When it was over, we were exhilarated and tired.

After that trip, I knew there had to be another way that would set people free without such taxing effort. Then it happened. I was teaching a series of classes on deliverance at a church, and we broke into small groups and began to minister to each other. As I was overseeing each group, my husband, who partners with me in ministry, was sitting on the platform stairs with his eyes closed, talking to the Lord. He felt the Lord sit next to him on the steps. The Lord lovingly said, "You know, there is an easier way."

Robert opened his eyes and he saw the people as the Lord saw them. They were beloved little children, approximately five or six years old. Each had their sword and was practicing sword-fighting the enemy. What he saw was precious. Yet the Lord said, "There is a better way."

Later, when Robert shared with me what the Lord had said to him, I was overjoyed and immediately began to pursue the Lord; I wanted to know this better way.

I have to laugh when I think about this because I had been doing this better way all along and not recognizing it for what it truly is. We now know: spiritual body mapping!

I will get into spiritual body mapping later in the book, but for now, I want to answer some frequently asked questions.

CHAPTER 2

POWER OF THE ENEMY

Whom Does the Enemy Target?

> And the LORD God said to the woman, "What is
> this you have done?" The woman said, "The serpent
> deceived me, and I ate." So the LORD God said to
> the serpent: Because you have done this, you are
> cursed more than all cattle, and more than every
> beast of the field; on your belly you shall go, and
> you shall eat dust all the days of your life. (Genesis
> 3:13-14 NKJV)

As most of us know, this passage is referring to the coming of the
Lord Jesus Christ and how He will crush the power of the enemy.
But when we look at the Hebrew, the scripture reveals much more.

> And I will put enmity[1] [hate] between you and the
> woman, and between your seed[2] [posterity] and
> her seed [posterity]. He shall bruise[3] [overwhelm]
> your head[4] [chief, authority]. And you shall bruise
> [overwhelm] His heel [rear of the army[5].]. (Gen.
> 3:15 NKJV)

The Lord was telling us this whole time who the enemy is going to target—the straggler!

Now take Gen. 3:15 through the cross to Matt. 12:43-45. We should look at everything in the Old Testament through the cross and view it from the New Testament side. What I mean by this is because of what Jesus did on the cross, dying for our sins, we are now under grace and not under the Old Testament Law. Therefore, we should examine how the New Testament and grace portrays the same matter. Because when we do, one of three things will happen:

1. The New Testament will change the matter.
2. The New Testament will fulfill the matter.
3. The New Testament leave the matter the same.

Please note: In Matt. 12:43-45, the spirit has not been "cast out." Spirits can come and go at will and spirits do not like to inhabit a person alone; they like to bring others more horrific than themselves in with them. Their objective is to "kill, steal, and destroy." If they cannot get that done, they will be satisfied with just capping you, where you feel like you can't seem to get past an invisible barrier, so you are ineffective for the Kingdom of God. Have you ever felt like you can get just so far and then you hit an invisible wall? The enemy has capped you. However, you have authority over this blockage! Use your God delegated power and the Word of the Lord against the enemy and cast it away from you.

For several years, I used to cast spirits into dry, empty places until one day it this practice backfired on me. There was a couple in ministry who were staying in their trailer outside my home while they ministered in different churches in our area. One day, I had performed a deliverance and told the spirits they had to go into dry, empty places and not to return. I also told them not to come back, because spirits often step outside only to then step right back in; they are very legalistic.

That night, when the couple returned, they walked into their trailer and chaos erupted. To say the least, it scared them, as the spirits ran out of the trailer, knocking things over in their wake. Unbeknownst to me, they had turned off the water to the trailer so it would not leak. Therefore, it was dry and uninhabited. It fit the criteria I had given the spirits. They just stepped outside and made themselves at home inside my friends' trailer. What an experience. I have since changed where I send them.

> When an unclean spirit goes out of a man, he goes through dry places, seeking rest[6] [recreation–], and finds none. Then he says, 'I will return to my house[7] [dwelling place–] from which I came." And when he comes, he finds it empty[8] [leisure, holiday–], swept[9] [to trail, root Greek word for swept, to choose oneself–], and put in order[10] [root Greek word for order: "to be carried off, the world"]. (Matt. 12:43 NKJV)

In Genesis 3, the verse specified that the target of the enemy would be the straggler. Matthew elaborates this further. In verse 44, we see what gives access to the enemy, "a person who trails behind, thinks only of him or herself and is carried off by the world." By allowing oneself to get caught up in the world, whether through compromised morals or with the "cares of the world," one permits legal access, doorways for the evil spirit to bring far worse than himself to "his dwelling place." Note the possessiveness, the feeling of ownership the demon exhibits toward "his person" in Matthew, the spirits feel they own the person they are tormenting.

> Matt. 12:45: "Then he goes and takes with him seven (seven in the Greek, means complete) other spirits more wicked than himself, and they enter and dwell there; and the last state of that man is worse than the first. So shall it also be with this wicked generation" (NKJV).

Examining this verse through the cross did not change or delete what Genesis defined. The enemy will target those who are trailing behind, thinking of themselves, and have been caught up in the things or cares of this world.

The question arises, Can a Christian be tormented by an evil spirit? "The Assemblies of God maintains that it is not possible for a Christian to be demon-possessed."[11] Absolutely correct! The controversy boils down to definitions and miscommunication. Firstly, one would need to define *a Christian*. According to Prince, "The term Christian means different things to different people… but most agree it is an individual who has repented for one's sins and through faith has received Jesus Christ as one's Savior."[12] To be *possessed* is to be owned and for Satan to own a Christian is ridiculous, as Jesus paid and redeemed the Christian with His own life, meaning the Christian is now owned by Jesus. The term *to possess* an evil spirit is different from *being possessed* by an evil spirit. This word comes from the Greek word *diamonizo*, which means "subject to demonic influence."[13] Whether a spirit is on the inside of a person or on the outside, the result is the same—the person is in a state of temptation, torment or spiritual blindness.

HIERARCHY OF THE ENEMY

To more fully understand the enemy's authority and ranks, let us look at a word study of Ephesians 6:10–18.

Finally, my brethren, be strong in the Lord and in the power of His might.

Put on the whole armor of God, that you may be able to stand against the wiles[14] [trickery-] of the devil.

For we do not wrestle[15] [the word 'wrestle' goes to a Greek root word that means "I exist"] against flesh and blood, but against principalities,[16] [chief-] against powers,[17] [delegated authority-], against the rulers of the darkness of this age[18] [leaders controlled by the enemy who operate in spirit of error-], against spiritual hosts of wickedness in the heavenly places[19] [evil spirits who are not earth bound-]. (KJV)

As you can see, there are different ranks in the army of Satan.

1. The chief rulers. These spirits are not earthbound and oversee vast armies over countries.
2. The delegated authority." These spirits may or may not be earthbound, but carry out the commands of the chiefs.
3. The human leaders, who are controlled by a spirit of error.
4. The hosts of wickedness in the heavenlies. These are evil spirits who are not earthbound.

To more fully understand what the Word is referring to by the term *heavenlies*, we need to know the evil spirits have access to what is called the *second heaven*, that place between us here on earth and where the Lord resides. This is a very violent place; it is where spiritual wars are carried out. We read in Daniel, chapter 10 about a war in the heavenlies. It is good to note when doing a deliverance that a door to the second heaven can be opened, so it is very important to close this door at the end of a session.

We have no need to fear. We have authority delegated to us by Jesus to trample over all evil. Not only do we have delegated authority over these spirits but through prayer, the Lord will expose their tricks and give us His perspective of the battle.

In doing a word study using the Greek according to *Strong's Concordance*, for Luke 10:19, we see the Lord is actually revealing two different types of strategy of evil spirits—that of serpents and that of scorpions.

> Behold, I give you the authority[20] [delegated authority-] to trample[21] [root word: "to hit with a single blow"-] on serpents[22] [root word: "to gaze at something remarkable"-] and scorpions,[23] [to pierce, root word of scorpions: through the idea of concealment-] and over all the power[24] [miraculous power-] of the enemy, and nothing shall by any means hurt you. (Luke 10:19 NKJV)

In other words, Jesus is saying, "I have delegated my authority to you to strike the enemy with a single blow." He goes on to reveal the two traps the enemy will set.

The first one is that of the serpent. Have you ever seen a snake after a rabbit or small prey? The snake will catch the eye of the victim and get it to fix its sight on them, the snake will sway back and forth to mesmerize the prey, then it strikes. The enemy, too, will try to get you to fix your eyes on something evil and woo you into a trap!

The second tactic the enemy will use is that of the scorpion. The word in the Greek means "to pierce"; it goes to a root word meaning a "concealed trap." The enemy will lay a trap for you to fall into with the aim of piercing you. Ps 119:105: "Your word is a lamp to my feet. And a light to my path" (NIV). The Lord will illuminate your path. The Word of God will light our way when we obey the Lord's principles; it will also keep you out of trouble and safe from the traps of the enemy.

During my studies, I have found three different classifications of spirits:

1. Tempters. These are beings who will set you up in a situation to cause you to sin. Examples of spirits who fall into this category are seducing spirits, lust, adultery. These beings will use legal rights such as generational curses to tempt or seduce you into a trap. They will show you the alluring part of the sin without revealing the negative consequences of the action. They work with other spirits to set a person up to fall. Let me give you an example. An individual with the spirit of adultery walks into a bar. From across the room, this person locks eyes with another who also has a spirit of adultery. There is instant magnetism. The two spirits of adultery are brought together by a seducing spirit. The three spirits will make sure the two people are pulled together to carry out their evil intentions. While the spirits are at work, they will block the persons' conscience. The victims will not think about their families or the consequences an interlude may cause until afterward; then, a third spirit is given access to each person's conscience to bring in the next classification of spirit, that of tormentor; in this case, that spirit is guilt.

2. Tormentors. These are spirits who cause emotional pain such as sorrow, rejection, jealousy, or guilt. This spirit will browbeat a person to wear him or her down. Their whole objective is to cause the person to give up on life. They will work on a person night and day to accomplish their

evil purpose. The sting with this spirit is that "as a person thinks, so shall he be." In other words, being mentally beaten down physically affects us. Our negative thinking can have an adverse affect upon our endocrine system, which controls hormones in our body such as dopamine and serotonin; these are the "feel good" hormones. As we think negatively, these hormones begin to shut down or slow down the endocrine system until the hormones are shut down. It becomes a vicious cycle. Once this happens, the person will deal with health issues. The evil spirit's intention is to usher in the spirit of heaviness or depression, then thoughts of suicide, and ultimately the spirit of death.

3. Blinding Spirits. These spirits, to me, are the most difficult to expose and eliminate in a person. The individual who is dealing with this type of spirit cannot "see" that they have a problem. Examples of this kind would lying, self-righteousness, deception, and ungratefulness.

I recently ministered to a person who had come into agreement with a lie. A deceiving spirit told the person she needed to kill her husband, go to jail, and minister the gospel in prison. To us in the room who were working with her, it was obvious this was a lie right out of the pit of hell. She believed the Lord had told her she had a calling to a jail ministry. When a victim is unable to see, he or she is in deception, and then it is hard to get the spiritually blinded person delivered.

How the Enemy Can Gain Access

We have already read in Gen. 3 and Matt. 12 whom the enemy targets. Now let us look at how he can gain access into our lives.

1. Believe a Lie.

   The first way for a spirit to gain entrance for harassment is for you to believe a lie you heard either through another person or through a thought dropped into your consciousness by a demon. Lies are the enemy's most vital weapon against us. Let's expose this deception; when a thought enters your head it will be in your thought voice and using the word *I*. In other words, the idea may come as "I am tired today" or "I feel lonely," etc. Do you see the deception? The use of the word *I* makes you think it is *you* who is thinking that thought. You are not! It is a subtle trick of the enemy for you to agree with, or not fight against, the idea. If that happens, then you will own whatever it is you are thinking. The question arises, How do I know if it is the enemy speaking to me? We will know them by their fruits. What would be the result of you not resisting that thought? Is it negative? Or would it be the fruit of the Holy Spirit that is listed in Galations 5:22? That will tell you who is talking.

   The Bible states in James 4:7, "Resist the devil and he will flee from you" (NIV). We as believers are to control our thoughts and not let our thoughts or emotions control us. Rom. 12:2: "And be not conformed to this world: but be ye transformed by the renewing of your mind, that ye may prove what is that good, and acceptable, and perfect, will of God" (KJV). It is up to us to renew our minds by the Word of God. If you have believed a lie, be quick to repent! Pray this prayer, "Father, forgive me for believing such and such lie. I ask for the belt of Truth to be activated so that I may be able to discern the lie from the truth, amen."

2. Unforgiveness.

The second area is huge in the spirit world and carries severe consequences. Unforgiveness is a massive door to the enemy in an individual's life. The disciples asked the Lord how to pray. Jesus in the Lord's Prayer equates our forgiveness of others with His forgiveness of us.

Luke 11:2: "And he said unto them, When ye pray, say, Our Father, which art in heaven, Hallowed be thy name. Thy kingdom come. Thy will be done on earth, as in heaven. Give us day by day our daily bread. And forgive us our sins; for we also forgive every one that is indebted to us. And lead us not into temptation; but deliver us from evil." (NKJV)

If we cannot forgive others, then we cannot expect the Lord to forgive us. I have had people tell me, "I do not have unforgiveness toward anyone."

I will then change my words and ask the person, "Are your feelings hurt right now?"

The answer invariably will be, "Yes ... so and so hurt my feelings over such and such." That is unforgiveness hidden behind hurt feelings.

Then on top of it all, when we hold unforgiveness in our hearts, it brings separation between the Father and us! Unforgiveness is a sin.

3. Unconfessed Sin.

The third area is unconfessed sin. Secrets are nasty little packages that hold an evil power—legal rights for the enemy to infiltrate. I would advise caution as to whom you confess your sin. My advice would be to confess your sin to your pastor. He will be able to assist in walking you through repentance and renouncing the hold the enemy may have over you through the situation.

Unconfessed sin holds power. The enemy can use the spirit of fear against you, fear that you will be "found out." I know a man who had an affair. After a short period, he broke off the relationship with the other woman and chose to give his life to the Lord Jesus Christ. He cried out for forgiveness and the Lord gave it to him. But the other woman kept calling him, "just to stay friends." These calls would vex his spirit, but he was afraid to tell the woman to quit calling lest she contact his wife. This situation went on for three years, the man being in sheer torment from the fear. He continued to ask the Lord for help. One day, the woman called, and the wife saw the call. The Lord had answered the man's prayers—he uncovered the enemy! The husband and wife stood together and wrote a note telling the other woman to go and not to bother him again. The enemy was exposed, the marriage healed, and peace prevailed. Now *that* is God!

4. Trauma.

Through trauma, spirits can enter. I was in a deliverance with a young bull rider. As soon as he sat down and said the renunciation prayer, his head fell forward, and when he lifted it back up, it was not him looking at us; it was an evil spirit. This spirit had entered him when he had been knocked out riding a bull in a rodeo. The spirit's goal was to kill him. In fact, during the session, he tried to throw the young man through a large glass window. After much ado, we finally got the spirit out, and when we did, the young man's head fell forward again, and this time, when he lifted it up, it was the young man himself looking back at us. He asked, "When are we going to start?" We all grinned. At that point, I began to realize that demons occupy different aspects of our consciousness. This demon was in the man's subconscious. The spirits can hear and obey even though they may be residing in the subconscious.

As I have previously stated it is important to make sure it is a deliverance the person needs and to know the difference between the spiritual and the soul realms. The soul is the mind, will, and emotions. A trauma victim may need a good Christian counselor to get through their ordeal. If you mistakenly use the incorrect route with this individual, it can cause stress as the person tries harder and harder to "hear" God or receive their healing. It can lead to thoughts that God does not love them, or their faith is not good enough.. Allow the victim to talk about their experiences and connect them with others in the body of Christ who have encountered similar experiences. Do not place them with someone who has no experience in their area of victimization. I have heard some crazy advice in such situations.

Something to note regarding trauma, and its effect in the spirit realm on an individual. Trauma can set a person up for "soul-ties." These soul ties can develop when two people experience a traumatic situation. For example, if two police officers work together and face a shoot-out, then a soul tie could develop between the two individuals. The situation would bond the two people together as they relied on each other for their lives. I will address soul-ties more in depth in a later chapter.

5. Altered State of Mind.

A spirit can enter a person through an altered state of mind. An altered state of mind would be anything that causes you to be out of control. Examples of this would be drinking enough alcohol to become intoxicated. Some friends of mine went out to dinner at a public steakhouse. The waiting area was next to the bar. As he and his wife sat there, a man who had been drinking at the bar fell off of his stool; he was out cold, totally inebriated. My friend watched as a demon walked across the room, looked down at him, laid himself on top of the man, then melted into his body. It was a terrible sight to behold.

Mind-altering drugs will do the same thing. A person's defenses are down, and the enemy can have access through that door.

6. Curses.

There are different types of curses. I will address a few of them in this book. The first one is a generational curse.

Ex. 34:7: "Keeping mercy for thousands, forgiving iniquity and transgression and sin, by no means clearing the guilty, visiting the iniquity of the fathers upon the children and the children's children to the third and the fourth generation." (NKJV)

Curses will set a pattern in a bloodline to be carried out according to whatever sin let it in. Have you ever noticed how some families are inclined to be sick, or die at a young age? If there is a pattern in the family line, it is wise to investigate where the curse entered the bloodline. Then have the individual repent for the sins of their forefathers and cover the situation in the blood of Jesus. You do not have to accept these bloodline curses you have spiritual authority to break and loose the curse from the individual and family line. But do not stop there. Loose the blessings of the Lord that were bottlenecked and choked off from flowing through the later generations.

The second curse is a word curse. These are words directed against you, your family line, or by you against yourself. Let me explain this a bit further. People are spirit beings. Spirit beings are creative with their words. The Father in heaven created the world by speaking it into being. The word tells us to call that which is not into being.

A good example of cursing oneself would be a woman who is unhappy with her weight and begins to call herself "fat." That woman may develop a problem losing the desired weight. She has given legal access through her words for spirits to tempt her to eat the wrong things and to cause her body to come into alignment with her thinking and words.

To break a word curse:

a. You need to forgive the person who cursed you, even if they have passed away, and even if that person is yourself.

b. Forgive anyone else you consider who was in the situation, including if you are blaming the Lord.

c. If you have taken any action against a person, then you need to repent for your actions and your words spoken against them.

7. Curses on Time.

Many years ago, I used to train horses, and I went through a period every November for three years when one of my horses would die. I did not understand, so I went to the Lord about it and cried out for help. He showed me there was a curse on time against my animals. Immediately, I took authority over it, repented for any sin, knowingly or unknowingly, that would have allowed the curse, and commanded the curse to be broken. I prayerfully covered each day of that month. The following year, when November came around, I prayed every day for the Lord's protection over our people, ranch, and horses. From that day on we have not experienced that curse.

A while back, I had a dream about a friend of mine. In the dream, she walked into my bedroom, into the bathroom, and the dream goes on... The interpretation of the dream was that she needed to repent for something that had allowed a legal spiritual action. I was later to find out what she needed to repent for that had opened a door to the enemy. My friend was suffering from cancer. One morning, she called me; the voice on the other end of the line was excited and full of amazement. My friend had had a revelation, and she made a point of telling me to share this revelation with others.

Her story goes like this. Her husband had passed away and at the graveside, she uttered the words, "I'll be with you soon." In my friend's mind, she was not thinking of dying; she was thinking of the immanent rapture. She had totally forgotten she had even thought those words let alone spoken them.

While she was in prayer one day, the Lord reminded her of those fateful utterings. She asked the Lord, "Why have You not honored my repentance of saying such a thing?"

The Holy Spirit answered her, "I know about the words spoken at the gravesite." And He showed her that her timing is not God's timing. Eccl 3:2-8 speaks of timing. She had cursed time, and that was the entry to the enemy in her life. It was not the words that allowed the enemy access; it was the cursed time. By uttering the words referring to time, she had put time into Satan's hands, and it had become defiled for her. She repented of what she had spoken and broke the curse on time.

I want to say that there is a flip-side to time. It can also contain God's blessings. Being in the correct timing and or season can place you smack dab in the middle of a "God thing."

Acts 3:10-11: "Then they knew that it was he who sat begging alms at the beautiful Gate of the temple; and they were filled with wonder and amazement at what had happened to him. Now as the lame man who was healed held onto Peter and John, all the people ran together to them in the porch which is called Solomon's, greatly amazed" (NKJV). The word *beautiful* in verse ten goes to a word that means "timely." At the right time, the lame man was healed.

Rom. 10:15: "And how shall they preach unless they are sent? As it is written: 'How beautiful [timely] are the feet of those who preach the gospel of peace, who bring glad tidings of good things" (NKJV). Again, the word *beautiful* goes to a Greek word that means "timely." So we can see that time can contain the blessings of the Lord!

8. Gates.

Gates are doors for spiritual travel. These gates can be located in the heavenlies, on earth, or under the earth.

Genesis 28:12 speaks of Jacob's ladder and the angels ascending and descending on the earth. This ladder is a heavenly gate and earthly gate.

The spiritual gates that are said to be "under" the earth have puzzled me. Many times, when I have seen a spirit and rebuked it, I have seen it dive into the ground. Not understanding this, I asked the Lord about it.

A few days later, I heard the Lord say, "There are gates under the ground." My brain froze. *Really?* Immediately I grabbed my Bible to confirm what I had heard. Phil 2:10: "That at the name of Jesus every knee should bow, of those in heaven, and of those on earth, and of those under the earth" (NKJV).

These gates can be a positive or a negative to people, places, or things. Evil spirits can use them to gain entrance into your house, property, anything under your authority. But for the purpose of this study, let us focus on how we can use them to further the kingdom of God. The purpose of a gate is to expedite a working access to and with God. The Lord wants a close and intimate working relationship with His people.

My husband had a revelation the other day. He said, "You know in the Old Testament when the people of God had to handle the ark with great care? They used poles and rings so as not to touch the holiness of God. Using the poles and rings kept them from being killed. This situation seems out of character for a loving God. It is not God's character to say, 'Don't touch me or I will annihilate you!'"

No! If you read and understand the character of God, then you will see that God is love, and He loves us so much He wants to be with us. He craves to be with us. After all,

25

God created man in the Garden to commune with Him. However, He is also aware of how dangerous His holiness can be to us (how fragile we are); therefore, he built a way for us to be with him—the rings and rods on the ark—Jesus Christ!

Hosea 4:6: "My people are destroyed for lack of knowledge." (KJV) We need to learn about these gates and understand God's purpose for them. I have counted many different gates in the Bible. We need to learn about these gates so that we can work with God and not against what He is doing. According to Psalms 115:16, He has given us dominion here on Earth. We are to be stewards over things in this world, which include spiritual gates. We are to guard these accesses, so they do not become defiled. In a session, it is important to address any defiled gates around a person. We are to clean and protect these gates to ensure their proper use. He has designed these gates specifically for spiritual travel.

Ps 24:7-8: "Lift up your heads, O ye gates; and be ye lift up, ye everlasting doors; and the King of glory shall come in. Who is this King of glory? The LORD is strong and mighty; the LORD is mighty in battle." (KJV)

Ps 78:23: "Though he had commanded the clouds from above, and opened the doors of heaven." (KJV)

There are geographical locations that have anointed gates on them. When the Lord was talking with Elijah, he told him to travel to Mt. Horeb/Mt. Sinai, where He would speak to him further (1 Kings 19:11-18). Jerusalem has a gate. Both David and Isaiah said that Jerusalem is the center of the earth. Jesus is coming through the eastern gate.

People have asked me, "What does it feel like when you are at the entrance of a gate?" There is a difference in the atmosphere. One thing I have noticed about gates is that there seems to be activity. In Gen 28:17 (Jacob's ladder), the Lord told Jacob that He would multiply him. There is an anointing for promotion here. What does anointing mean? To smear oil, to consecrate. At a gate, your consecration and purpose with the Lord may be increased and/or directed.

Remember that in Daniel Chapter Ten, Daniel was on his face twenty-one days while a battle raged above him. The battle was in the heavenlies; Gabriel had to call Michael for help to break through the enemy's lines to deliver the message from the Lord to Daniel. Looking at Daniel and understanding what David and Isaiah stated about Jerusalem, we can see that the enemy indeed seeks to block a gate.

In the Kingdom of God, we have authority and dominion on earth! It is our job to see that we steward these gates and pray according to the will of the Father. We are to ensure consecrated access through our prayers. We are to hear from the Lord through the Holy Spirit and pray as He directs.

How do we Open Gates?

First, let me point out one thing, the Holy Ghost-baptized believer *always* has an open heaven. For the Holy Spirit is a direct link to the throne room of God. He resides within you. And He will direct your path. But there are some things I should point out.

1. The Archangel Gabriel told Daniel, "The Lord heard you from the time you set your mind…" The key to opening gates is to make up your mind and stay determined in the spirit–you will get the Lord's attention. Determination and spiritual warfare will open gates.

2. Acts 2:1, Unity opened a door to the Holy Spirit when the one hundred twenty were all in one accord and one place. Unity ushered in the Holy Spirit and brought the baptism of empowerment.

3. Ps 141: 2-3: "Let my prayer be set forth before thee as incense; and the lifting up of my hands as the evening sacrifice. Set a guard, O LORD, before my mouth; keep the door of my lips" (NKJV). Our faith-filled words will create gates. God spoke and created the world; scientists have proven rocks hold sound, and the universe itself contains sound. Scientists have found radio waves in space from years ago. Sound is huge in opening and closing doors between the heavenlies, Earth and below.

4. Prayer and Fasting will open gates. Remember that in Daniel Chapter 10, he was praying and fasting when Gabriel appeared to him with the answers he was seeking. Prayer will open eyes to "see" into the spirit realm. In 2 Kings 8-17, When Elisha prayed, his servant saw the angels ready to fight for them. Visions, dreams, and trances also open eyes to see into the heavenlies. In another situation, Daniel fell into a dream/trance and saw the angel Gabriel. Again, Peter fell into a trance on the rooftop in Acts 11:5 and saw a sheet let down from heaven.

5. Faith-filled Worship will open gates into the heavenlies. Psalms 22:3: "Yet you are enthroned as the Holy One; you are the one Israel praises" (NIV).

Other gates worthy of mention:

Ps 118:19-20: The gate of righteousness is called the Gate of the Lord that the righteous shall enter through.

Matt 7:13 talks about the strait gate in which the children of the Lord shall enter. Strait means a narrow passage between obstacles…few shall find it.

1 Cor 16:9: Paul talks about a "great and effective" door for ministry; then he goes on to state that this door is opened only by the Lord in 2 Cor 2:12.

So we see there are gates we can open, and there are doors only the Lord opens. When we do open a door, we must make sure to open it into the throne room of God and not into somewhere else. Again I want to remind you that in deliverance, it is easy to open a door to the heavenlies and forget to close it. That is when you get demonic traffic. Close the gates after a session.

Another warning: Be aware that witches can open gates on your land. I was visiting a friend in northern California. I was sitting at his picnic table and noticed a spiritual gate. I did not say anything at the time. A few months passed and I received a phone call from him. He had just encountered a demon and wanted to tell me what happened. I knew then that the timing was right to tell him about the gate on his property. He asked what the location was to the gate, and I told him to the north and described exactly where it could to be found. He explained to me that this area bordered the property of his neighbor who was a practicing witch. I told him how to close the demonic gate by declaring it closed and calling on the blood of Jesus Christ to cover it. He did as instructed and experienced no more demonic encounters.

9. Godly Soul Ties vs. Ungodly Soul Ties; Godly Soul Ties vs. Friendship Soul Ties.

There are definitely "Godly Soul Ties" mentioned in the Old Testament as well as in the New Testament. We need to nurture these soul ties. The first that comes to mind is the Godly relationship between Jonathan and David, this tie was a "friendship tie."

> 1 Sam. 18:1-3: "Now when he had finished speaking to Saul, the soul of Jonathan was knit to the soul of David, and Jonathan loved him as his own soul. Saul took him that day, and would not let him go home to his father's house anymore. Then Jonathan and David made a covenant because he loved him as his soul" (KJV).

When David was at home with his father, the prophet Samuel had anointed him king of Israel. David slew Goliath as the anointed king of Israel.

The soul tie between Jonathan and David was a Godly knitting of the two souls as it positioned David for preparation to become king of Israel. David's relationship with Jonathan afforded his training in court protocol and as a military leader.

Husband and Wife Soul Ties (Blood Covenants)

> Eph. 5:31: "For this reason a man shall leave his father and mother and be joined to his wife, and the two shall become one flesh" (NKJV).

When a man and woman marry, they each are a part of making a whole unit. The Lord knits them together into "one flesh." This covenant is one of the strongest ties there is as it involves what is called *a blood covenant*. When a woman has sexual intercourse for the first time, her hymen is broken, and she will shed blood, thereby sealing the union in a blood covenant.

A Godly marriage between a husband and a wife is a parable for all the world to see the intimate relationship the Lord would like to have with His people. He too has a blood covenant with us in that Jesus, part of the God-head, shed His blood for the forgiveness and remission of our sins. When we accept Him as our Savior, we come into this blood covenant with Him.

A blood covenant can be done with other people, as well, creating a soul tie with that person. Many native tribes practice this in forming alliances.

Ungodly Soul Ties; Sexual Soul Ties

In deliverance, we must make sure to address ungodly soul ties. In the spirit realm, the soul ties I have seen look similar to an umbilical cord in which demons can transfer from one person to the next. Let me give an example of how this would work. Let's say a couple had sex when they were young, then life takes them on different paths, and they marry other people. The previous soul tie remains. It will set the marriages up for failure.

A good analogy is to take two pieces of wet paper, stick them together, and let them dry. After they have dried, try pulling them apart; it does not work. They will tear and leave pieces behind. The same goes for soul ties. The people with these ties are not whole. You have heard people say, "I left part of myself with her." They did leave part of the soul with that person. There is access through soul ties into the soul realm. Not only does the previous sex partner have ongoing access to this one person, but to their previous sex partners as well.

Mental Affairs

Even affairs of the mind can create soul ties. A man and woman may never actually have sex, but if they lean on each other, they may become each other's best friends. They may share more with each other and have a closer relationship than they do with their own spouses. Acting in this manner with each other is a perfect set-up for an ungodly soul tie.

Trauma Soul Ties

Trauma can cause a soul tie with a person as well. In traumatic situations there is a bond that can develop between two people and weld them together; that is a soul tie. An example of such a tie would be seen in the case of police officers. Working closely with partners, they have to face high-stress situations frequently. These people must develop a close relationship in which they trust each other with their lives.

Substance Abuse Soul Ties

Recently, I received a phone call, and the person on the other end asked if it was possible to develop a "soul tie" to another person by doing drugs with them. This person went on to explain that there were times when he would be going about his own business and out of the blue he would have this incredible desire to do drugs. It unnerved him.

In his case, I knew we had already kicked out the spirits associated with drugs (spirit of bondage, addiction, Python, the spirit that will cause a person to return to drug addiction, etc.) I also knew they may return to "test the waters." But, after talking more with him, I began to discern that he was experiencing the activity of a "soul tie."

I told him we would break it right then and there on the phone. The person repented for the sin of doing the drugs as well as of doing them with this other person. We severed the soul tie and commanded all works of it null and void in his life. He felt something lift off and immediately felt lighter.

Location Soul Ties

A person can develop direct soul ties through memories that link him or her to an item, place, or a person. How do you know if you have a location soul tie? When you think of a place or a thing, does it tie you to someone with whom you committed a sin? If you answered, "yes," then the tie needs to be broken.

When I was a young woman, I would wake up at night after a dream of a place my family had in Montana, and I would be terribly homesick. I would feel actual pain in my heart and an incredible yearning to go back. It was many years later that I learned about geographical soul ties. These are soul ties that link us to a place. I learned that this feeling of wishing to return to Montana was not a leading from the Holy Spirit by examining the fruit of the situation.

1. It did not bring peace
2. It did not lead me to the Lord–on the contrary, it would lead me away from His ministry
3. It would have caused problems in my marriage
4. It did cause confusion, pain, and sickness

Some people experience these ties and their effects even when they have not visited an area. That kind of manifestation more than likely involves a "familiar spirit" who is around the person. The spirit has visited that location and is trying to draw the person there.

You must examine the fruit of the spirit to know if it is the Lord leading you or an evil spirit. If it is an evil soul tie, you will break it the same way you break a tie between you and another person. But also, be sure to cleanse the land; there may be a sin issue involved.

Breaking a Soul Tie

1. Repent of the sin and action it took to create it
2. Renounce the soul tie and cut it in the name of Jesus Christ
3. Render its works null and void
4. Be sure to use the blood of Jesus to cleanse the wound and whatever situation allowed the ungodly soul tie to develop and then seal it.

CHAPTER 3

LESSER-KNOWN SPIRITS

I included this chapter to reference spirits about whom I have not found too much information and to make some observations on the spirits from my experience in this type of ministry.

When I first started in deliverance, there were not many of us brave or, as I laughingly say, "foolish" enough to get involved in deliverance. At the time, people were afraid of this practice. There was a notion that if you spoke Satan's name, he would appear, so people just basically ignored the obvious. Christians were sitting in the church pews in torment and pain. Where was the manifestation of "those He sets free, ye are free indeed"?

Throughout the years of working in ministry I gained some understanding.

1. A spiritual door can open through a seducing spirit. This spirit is not necessarily what you think. It seduces you into compromising or becoming complacent. When we compromise our morals, beliefs, etc., the seducing spirit enters and puts his foot in the door to hold it open for a stronger spirit to enter. Unforgiveness will throw the door wide open. So look for this spirit when you are in a session; as

a seducing spirit is usually the first to enter when temptation spirits are present.

2. When confronted with spirits who are combative, I have learned not to fight back—that is what they want you to do. There is a much more powerful weapon—love.

One day, I walked into the church where my husband and I pastor, and several of our prayer partners were in a deliverance with a young man who was in his twenties. The young man was violent, and the men were on the floor holding him so he could not hurt anyone. The Lord quickened my spirit to go to the young man and tell him about Jesus's love. As I spoke about the love of the Lord, everything quieted down, and the spirits left. I realized the spirits could not fight the love of the Lord! It appeared to be like a vapor or fog to them; they could not grasp the concept of love. The greatest weapon you have in deliverance is love.

Spiritual Orphans

Sitting at the kitchen table one day, I heard the Lord say, "We create spiritual orphans." I thought, *Really, Lord? How are we creating spiritual orphans?* He began to show me through the scriptures His love for the widow and orphan. As I read, I realized He wasn't just referring to them in the natural sense. He opened my eyes to those around me who felt left out no matter how hard we tried to include them. There was a type of disconnect these people experienced in the body of Christ.

I noted that during counseling, these people seemed to have tremendously deep heart wounds. Rejection played a big part in their lives and because of this, they would throw up walls around themselves, hoping to protect their heart from any further pain. Two different spirits instigated this, rejection and fear. These two spirits team up to build walls and ultimately a fortress. The person may want to fit in but will reject others before they themselves are rejected—hence, the disconnection from the group.

An orphan may manifest a few different characteristics, all of which they are hoping to use to fill the void or pain in their lives. According to Donna Kazenske, they will manifest in the following ways:

1. Material things (power through prestige)
2. Addiction (anesthetizes their pain)
3. Power through position (they are seeking acceptance and validation)[25]

An orphan may come across as controlling. The need to control arises out of the need to protect their situation. The spirit of fear will try to control them so that no one can get too close.

The Word states that we are to love His people; that means we are to serve each other and desire their needs over our own. We need to recognize the spiritual orphans in our midst and reach out to them. Yes, they come with baggage, but didn't we all?

> Pure religion and undefiled before God and the Father is this, To visit[26] (to watch, like a scout-) the fatherless and widows in their affliction, and to keep himself unspotted from the world. (James 1:27 KJV)

Obviously, there is more than one type of orphan— a natural orphan as well as a spiritual orphan, and I believe the Lord would have us reach out to both.

Alters (Demons)

In the ministry of deliverance, we have discovered *alters*. They are not to be confused with familiar spirits.

The alters I am referring to are not splinters—that is to say, splinters of the mind. Alters are very intriguing; in fact, they do not know they are demons. They resent it if you call them by that term. They usually have a human name. They do not seem to have any memory of before living in their present individual, whom they call their 'house'. They can be any age. They can grow and develop with the person they are connected to, or they can grow during a certain period and stop while the person continues to age.

They can come in due to trauma or by being *planted*. In the occult, demons are planted in individuals with triggers that activate the desired response. I know of one person who had an alter planted so that if she ever tried to run away from her family, all her mother had to do was send her a letter with a particular picture on it. That picture was the trigger that told the alter to go into action and bring her home. The girl was powerless to resist. If the person who has an alter does try to resist, the alter may become aggressive to get its way.

The alter believes it is there to help or protect the person it is living within. Did you have a pretend friend when you were young? Make-believe playing can be an easy door for an alter to gain access.

They always will build a *house* within their human. That house can be absolutely anything. We have run across houses that were refrigerators, boxes, a castle, etc. It is crucial to open them and look inside the house. Be sure to visit each room as you may find other spirits, alters, wounds, hurtful memories. The spiritual house the alter may have built can contain weapons, doors, the list is endless, all of which, must be destroyed along with all of its contents. The destruction of the spiritual house is necessary because, if left intact, it can become a door later for spirits to enter.

To cast this spirit out, you need to identify the circumstances in which it gained access. This process may mean time-traveling—taking the person back in time to a situation that was traumatic and learning where the spirit entered or had legal access. We do this in almost every deliverance. Sometimes, we have to go through many generations to get to the root of a sin in the family line in order to get an alter or various spirit(s) dislodged.

I remember that in one case we went back to the year 1742. Apparently, there had been a pirate in the bloodlines of this individual and the sins of the forefathers had manifested in this man today. Once we went back to the root of the sin, exposed it, and he repented of the lie this individual had believed as well as any unforgiveness and negative actions, we called on the blood and name of Jesus, and then the power of the alter was broken. We then destroyed its house.

When dealing with an alter, I have found it helpful to show it that the person it inhabits is now in the hands of the Holy Spirit. Sharing this knowledge seems to ease the fight in getting it out. Sometimes they do not know how to leave. Therefore, we will create a door for them to leave through. You can do this by simply speaking a door into existence. There are times we will ask angels to assist. Once the alter leaves, and the spiritual house is destroyed, it is important to fill the person with the Holy Spirit, this will ensure a supernatural power to withstand the enemy.

Be aware, the person who had the alter may go through what seems to be mourning the loss of the alter. The alter may have been a security blanket. You will need to encourage to the person to look to the Holy Spirit for comfort and protection.

Spirit of Cancer

I have to tell you what the Lord showed me about that particular spirit. Both my mentors passed away from cancer within three months of each other. I was furious and told the Lord exactly what I thought about that awful situation. I prayed and asked Him for the key to destroy that particular spirit. All of a sudden, the wall in my living room turned into a home theater, and I saw what appeared to be an ant or some creature with a segmented body. It wore over its back what looked like an impenetrable, smooth shell. It was gigantic and crawled up my wall. I asked the Lord, "What is it?"

He said, "That is the spirit of cancer."

I watched as this thing crawled straight, then started to turn, the shell lifting to reveal a vulnerable spot. I saw a sharp spear pierce the shell and enter the body, this stopped it.

Later, a couple of friends were visiting, and I shared the vision with them. I asked, "What would cause the thing to turn?"

Out of the husband's mouth came the profound answer. "What causes a *person* to turn around? Repentance!" Immediately, we had the wonderful revelation. At the moment of repentance, the spirit is vulnerable, and we can pierce it.

Once we received this revelation, we began to put it into practice. I remember three different cases that gave me quite an education.

Case #1. A couple called me and asked if I would meet with their grown daughter. I agreed. The three of them arrived at the appointed time. I looked at the daughter and heard the Lord say, "Don't touch her."

I was frantic and quickly asked the Lord, "What do I do now?" He had me talk with the mother and, through the conversation, I learned that she had unforgiveness toward her brother. After a few minutes of my ministering to her, she came to the place of forgiveness. Immediately, after she uttered the prayer of forgiveness, the Lord turned me to the father, who had been diagnosed with stage-3 lung cancer. I asked him, "Where is the cancer in your body?" He pointed to the area, and I laid my hands on it and began to rebuke it as though it were a demon.

He felt a lump move upward, this feeling startled him. It continued to move into his throat and out of his mouth. A week or two later, he went back to his doctor and upon further examination and tests—no cancer!

What did we learn from this? There is a mystery to marriage, as the Bible clearly states in Eph. 5:28-31:

> So ought men to love their wives as their own bodies. He that loveth his wife loveth himself. For no man ever yet hated his own flesh; but nourisheth and cherisheth it, even as the Lord the church: For we are members of his body, of his flesh, and of his bones. For this cause shall a man leave his father and mother, and shall be joined unto his wife, and they two shall be one flesh. (KJV)

What I learned was the fact that if one of the spouses holds unforgiveness, it can and will affect the mate. This theory has now been proven over and over in deliverance. In the above case, the wife held unforgiveness toward her brother and chose to forgive, and this released her husband from the spirit of cancer. As long as the wife kept her unforgiveness, the spirit had a legal right to stay. The man and woman are "one flesh."

Case #2. This was another husband and wife situation. They had gone through a terrible ordeal. The husband had developed colon cancer. We have learned that this ailment is rooted in a deep bitterness. He had forgiven the people who had brought so much

41

pain into his life, but the wife had not. In the end, he was not healed and passed away.

> Beloved, I wish above all things that thou mayest prosper and be in health, even as thy soul prospereth.
> (3 John 2 KJV)

Do you see the equal sign? It is in the word *even*. Your prosperity and health are connected to the way your soul prospers. The soul is your mind, will, and emotions. As your mind, will, and emotions become conformed to the image of Christ, good things are brought into your life.

Case #3, Again a husband and wife. The husband had brain cancer. As we began to pray for him, the Lord showed me that they were involved in a lawsuit. I have never been able to help anyone who is participating in a lawsuit. When I asked the Lord why that is, He showed me it has to do with the spiritual law of "binding and loosing." If one becomes the aggressor in such a dispute, this gives legal right to the enemy to protect itself and attack.

We must examine our motive. Why are you in a lawsuit? Is it for self? If so, then the motive will give legal rights to the enemy to take away from you later. People I have known who have sued someone later found themselves with pretty severe health issues.

I asked the Lord about a well-known Christian attorney, who is in court on a regular basis. How is it that he could sue and not have repercussions? The Lord quickly answered, "He is not demanding for himself, but he is fighting for the people." Do you see the difference in the motive? This attorney is a blessed man—and he should be. God bless him.

When I asked the couple about their legal action, they admitted to being involved in a class action suit against a public utility company. After I explained to them that I would not be able to help them as long as they were participating in this case, they both repented and agreed to drop the lawsuit. Immediately, we began the deliverance. Through the whole thing, I had a check in my spirit about the wife. Something was wrong, but I could not put my finger on it.

The husband went back to the doctors, and they were unable to find any tumors. He was healed. He and his wife were Catholic. To say the least, he had some questions, so he went to see his priest. His priest explained miracles to him. Much later, I found out that the tumors had returned. I asked a few questions, trying to find out what had happened. The wife had allowed unforgiveness back in and opened a door for legal access to the enemy.

Since then, I have learned something else about the spirit of cancer. It is linked very closely with a spirit by the name of *destroyer* (not destruction). Destroyer is the spirit that devours a person a piece at a time. If this spirit is not dealt with when you deal with cancer, more than likely the cancer will return. The same holds true when doing a deliverance on a person addicted to drugs. You need to cast out the spirit of bondage but make sure you get the Python spirit. It is Python that will cause them to fall back into drugs.

I remember a case of a young woman who had heard about our team and called for help. She had cancer, and it was all through her body. We had a session with her, and it seemed to help. A week or two later, her aunt called and asked to come up immediately as the young woman was in severe pain, so much pain that the morphine would not touch it and she was desperate for some relief. We agreed to meet with her.

As we were waiting for them to arrive, I went to the church and prayed. I had no idea what we were going to do and told the Lord so. He responded by having me mix four different oils together and told me to anoint this young woman with the oils.

I will never forget seeing the girl walk through the doors of the church that night. She was bent over and needed help to walk for the pain was great. My heart broke, and I was filled with compassion. My prayer partner and I prayed and anointed her with the four oils. Let me tell you what our father in heaven did—that girl literally danced out of the church that night. He set her free of the pain.

LEVIATHAN AND THE RIVER

I had a vision…I was walking up to a river. As I approached, I could smell the wonderful aromas of being near a woodsy river. I looked into the water and saw algae. I was confused; I asked what it was and saw an alligator. I asked what that was and heard he was the enemy that guards others against approaching the river. I saw his mouth and immediately bound the mouth of the enemy. I saw his scales and knew him to be thick skinned, I then saw his eyes. In fact, I met him eye to eye. I blinded him in Jesus's name. I looked back at the river. Now it had changed. I saw a broad river, and as I approached it was like I passed through a wall and the colors changed. They had darkened. I immediately heard "we look through a glass darkly," and I asked the Lord to illuminate the area and then I was taken to somewhere at the end of the river. I saw doors holding the water, and as I asked for illumination, the doors opened to a spillway and the beautiful clear water began to spill out…

The next day, I asked the Lord to take me back to the river. This time, I saw the river and could smell the wonderful woodsy aromas again, but when I looked into the river, I saw it was dark, this was good because according to Ps. 18:11, the darkness is the Lord's secret place. As I watched, I saw a yellow water lily rise out of the water and float on the surface.

In the next scene in the vision, I saw a hand, and it was reaching for a dial on a safe. I watched as it dialed the combination and the door swung open.

I went to the Bible to see if this is lined up with God's Word. Always test/try the spirit behind a vision. I interpreted the vision. The river in the vision is the river of revelation, the life that flows from heaven. The river had been stopped up by Leviathan, as mentioned in Job 41. It was Leviathan who came between Job and the Lord in communication this spirit uses gossip, slander, and lies. He has a tough hide and is not easily frightened, driven off, or killed. This spirit guards the river and tries to keep people from it.

The third part of the vision was of the darkened river again, but this time the Lord showed me that we look through a glass darkly. In other words, we need to ask the Lord to illuminate our understanding in order to discern. We are to pray for the floodgates of the river to open to us. Our tithes and offerings connect to the floodgates.

> "0 bring the whole tithe into the storehouse, that there may be food in my house. Test me in this," says the LORD Almighty, "and see if I will not throw open the floodgates of heaven and pour out so much blessing that you will not have room enough for it. I will prevent pests from devouring your crops, and the vines in your fields will not cast their fruit," says the LORD Almighty. "Then all the nations will call you blessed, for yours will be a delightful land," says the LORD Almighty." (Mal 3:10-12 NKJV)

The next day, I asked the Lord to take me back to the river. In this vision, the river was dark and the yellow lily arose once again.

The Lord showed me that the treasures of the Lord are hidden in the deep; that is, revelation for those who have a pure heart (Heb. 10:19-25) and who are God-like.

The vision of the dial, the Lord showed me, refers to the combination used to unlock the revelations from the river - those with a pure heart and God-like.

Just as Python guards the door to your next level or your new transition toward God, using discouragement, fear and things from your past to either tempt or torment you. Leviathan guards the river of life, using lies, gossip, strife, division and making a person feel like their communication with the Lord has been cut. When we want more revelation from the Lord, we will encounter this spirit.

It is important for us to seek out the river, for it is the river of life and it brings nourishment to us; we are as the trees, for we are to go out and heal the nations. In some places in the Bible, we are called oak trees, which means restoration.

1. Ps 36:8 brings delight, and from it we will see. It brings vision.
2. Ps 46:8 shows us that gladness and joy are in the river
3. Ps 105 brings life, salvation, and deliverance.
4. Ps 1:3 shows us that when we are planted near the water, we yield fruit in due season, do not grow faint, and we prosper.
5. Jer 2:13 says that He is the living water.
6. John 4:14 says that from the living water comes eternal life.
7. Ez 47 reveals that *river* comes from a root word meaning "inheritance."
8. Rev. 1:15 says that the voice of the Lord is as many waters.

Is it any wonder the enemy wants to keep you from the river of revelation?

According to Job 41, Leviathan's work can only be destroyed by the Word of the Lord. Leviathan is the king over the prideful, and he speaks slander, gossip, and lies. He watches. He strikes from behind, and you may not see the blow coming (Rev 12:4).

Jesus has given His authority to us. We have the Spirit of God, the Holy Spirit within us. Using the Word of God, we can defeat this enemy.

> In that day the LORD with his sore and great and strong sword shall punish leviathan the piercing[27] (run/fear)- serpent, even leviathan that crooked[28] (torturous) -serpent; and he shall slay the dragon that is in the sea (Is. 27:1 KJV).

The book of Isaiah reveals some of Leviathan's other traits. He causes people to run in fear, and in other situations he will torture or torment them. Therefore, Leviathan is the king of pride, who guards the river of revelation or life, and his manifestations are:

1. Gossip, slander, and lies
2. He will guard and watches for opportunity to strike
3. He strikes from behind, you may not see him coming
4. He uses fear to cause you to run
5. He uses torment

We are overcomers and more than conquerors in Jesus's name. We can defeat Leviathan through the blood of the lamb, the Word of God, and the power of our testimony.

PYTHON AND THE GATE

A while back, I went through three days of pure black heaviness. I cried at the drop of a hat, I wanted to crawl into a hole, and I am not typically a depressed person. It was quite abnormal for this to happen. On the third day, I'd had enough and put on worship music; that should have been my first action. Through the worship music, I received a breakthrough, and the heaviness came off. The Bible tells us to put on the garment of praise for the spirit of heaviness. Within a few minutes, I heard my Lord's voice say, "Tell the people at the door they will face fear, discouragement [heaviness], and their old demons [issues fought in the past]." At the door of your next transition into the Kingdom of God, you will face the spirit of Python.

Python's first and foremost objective is to keep you from attaining the promises or vision the Lord has given you. He will try to spiritually blind and suffocate you with heaviness. Just as a python snake in the natural world does to its victims, the spiritual python will squeeze ever so slightly with its victim's each breath. The victim does not know it is happening until it is too late and they are weighed down by depression.

This spirit will target leaders, as in the case of Num. 13:2. Here, the Israelites were positioned to move through the gate of their next transition. They sent out spies into the land. These spies were the heads of tribes and leaders. They came back with fear and discouragement, even after the Lord told them the land belonged to them. They could not "see" what the Lord was saying, they were focused on the problem, the giants, and because of this, they lost hope and vision. Only two of the spies focused on the blessings, the extraordinary size of the grapes. Because they believed God and focused on the blessings instead of the problem, they transitioned into the promised land.

Another case of the python spirit being drawn to leaders is in Acts 16:16-19:

> Now it happened, as we went to prayer, that a certain slave girl possessed with a spirit of divination met us, who brought her masters much profit by fortune-telling. This girl followed Paul and us, and cried out, saying, These men are the servants of the Most High God, who proclaim to us the way of salvation. And this she did for many days." (NKJV)

According to Strong's Concordance, the word Divination is: Puthon (*poo'-thone*) a python, inspiration (soothsaying) or witchcraft (Strong's Concordance). Python is behind witchcraft and divination.

When you are in a deliverance, and someone is being set free of drugs, you will want to address Python, along with the spirit of bondage and addiction, as well as the spirit of witchcraft (over pharmacia and sorcery). If you do not get Python out, he will hold the door open for the others to return.

How do you know if Python is active? The person will experience either some or all of the following symptoms:

1. Heavy weight on one's chest
2. Choking
3. Drugs/addiction
4. Divination (false prophesy)
5. Witchcraft (the word for pharmacy is connected to sorcery, i.e., witchcraft, ancient arts for alleviating pain, rebellion, control)
6. Loss of hope (Python squeezes the breath of God out of you)
7. Fear

8. Infirmity (sickness)

As I have already stated, I have encountered this spirit myself and let me tell you it was not fun. When Python is cast out, it can physically hurt. I remember feeling it run down my ribcage and painfully out my right hip. Knowing what I know now, I have to smile as I have learned what the right hip stands for in spiritual interpretation. The hip speaks of one's balance in life. At that time, I was totally out of balance. In fact, I was a full-blown workaholic, and this allowed access to that spirit!

So when dealing with Python, always remember, "What did God say?" Lay down those old things that hold you back from making the next transition in your life!

Spirit of Lawlessness

> But as to the Son, He says to Him, Your throne, O God, is forever and ever [to the ages of the ages], and the scepter of Your kingdom is a scepter of absolute righteousness [of justice and straightforwardness]. (Heb. 1:8 KJV)

> You have loved righteousness [You have delighted in integrity, virtue, and uprightness in purpose, thought, and action] and You have hated lawlessness (injustice and iniquity). Therefore God, [even] Your God, has anointed You with the oil of exultant joy and gladness above and beyond Your companions. (Heb. 1:9 KJV)

We see several attributes about Jesus that please the Father. Let's look at them:

1. His scepter is of righteousness (justice and straightforwardness)
2. He delights in righteousness (integrity, virtue and uprightness in purpose, thought and action)
3. He hates lawlessness (injustice & iniquity)
4. He is anointed with joy and gladness

The gospels talk about Jesus delegating His authority to us. We are His ambassadors while we are in this mortal body. Our physical body gives us the power to operate in the natural world. Once we shed our body, we will not be able to function in the natural world, as we will be a spirit. We must use this authority that Jesus has given us to complete our calling while we are still physically here.

What I wanted to point out in the above verse is the equal sign in verse 9. It is in the word *therefore*. Because Jesus loved righteousness and hated lawlessness, therefore God anointed Him with the oil of joy and gladness. So how do we apply this in our own lives? What exactly did He delegate to us? The first thing we will address is Jesus's scepter of righteous (justice and straightforwardness).

He has delegated us His spiritual authority with His scepter of right-standing with the Lord. He has redeemed us (paid for us, purchased us) by His blood and by applying that blood on the altar in heaven, justice is served. The wages of sin is death; Jesus paid for our sins with His life. Therefore, when we accepted Him as our Savior and asked forgiveness for our sins, his blood covered those sins and placed us in right-standing with the father in heaven.

Also connected with His scepter is straightforwardness and truth. Jesus makes this very clear:

> Then Jesus said to those Jews who believed Him, "If you abide in My word, you are My disciples indeed. And you shall know the truth, and the truth shall make you free. (John 8:31-32 NKJV)

> Therefore if the Son makes you free, you shall be
> free indeed. (John 8:36 NKJV)

As previously stated, Jesus delights in righteousness, which means: integrity, virtue, and uprightness in purpose, thought, and action. The Lord delights in integrity, which according to Webster's Dictionary means: the quality of being honest and having strong moral principles. .

> The integrity of the honest keeps them on track;
> the deviousness of crooks brings them to ruin. (Pr
> 11:3 NKJV)

A person of integrity is a person who can be trusted. He or she has a plumb line in their life and no matter what the circumstances are they are going to adhere to that plumb line.

> Then GOD said to Satan, "Have you noticed
> my friend Job? There's no one quite like him, is
> there—honest and true to his word, totally devoted
> to God and hating evil? He still has a firm grip on
> his integrity! You tried to trick me into destroying
> him, but it didn't work." (Job 2:3)

Why did God say that Job had a firm grip on his integrity? Because God knew Job's heart. Job was honest, true to his word, devoted to God, and hated evil. Circumstances did not change the way Job behaved. He was the same in the heat of his suffering as he was when things were good. Now *that* is character—God's character.

Jesus hates lawlessness (injustice and iniquity). 1 John 3:4 clearly defines lawlessness: "Whoever commits sin also commits lawlessness, and sin is lawlessness" (NKJV).

There are two commandments that are considered the most important—love your God with all of your heart and love your neighbor. Lawlessness is the polar opposite of these commandments. The manifestations of lawlessness is:

1. Cause love to grow cold, according to Matt 24:12
2. Cause a person to commit sin, according to 1 John 3:4
3. Deception hiding within a person's heart, according to Matt 23:28
4. Self-deception, according to Matt 7:23

Lawlessness is the anti-Christ spirit.

> The coming of the lawless one is according to the working of Satan, with all power, signs, and lying wonders, and with all unrighteous deception among those who perish, because they did not receive the love of the truth, that they might be saved. (2 Th. 2:9-10 NKJV)

So what is the remedy for lawlessness? To love the Lord with all of your heart and obey His commands. To allow the work of the Holy Spirit in your life. (2 Th 2:7)

I believe *some* people who suffer from depression, may have a hidden or unconfessed sin in their lives. There is a demonic power in keeping something secret. It gives that demon a right to torment you. The Bible states that we should confess our sins one to another— though please use discretion as to whom you choose to share your situation with. The Lord knew that confessing our sin to one another takes the power of control and fear away from the enemy and defeats his plan to destroy you. We are to drop sin and lawlessness like a hot potato. Run from the very appearance of evil.

Again, let's re-examine what this verse states about Jesus. He loves righteousness and He hates lawlessness, which means He is full of joy and gladness. If you are experiencing being unsettled, are not content in life, and things are just not right, then I am asking you to examine your life and see where the spirit of lawlessness might be hiding. Remember, he can hide and he is good at it. You may need to ask for help in this area, as he is also a master of deception. Again, the remedy for this spirit is the Holy Spirit.

> However, when He, the Spirit of truth, has come, He will guide you into all truth; for He will not speak on His own authority, but whatever He hears He will speak; and He will tell you things to come. He will glorify Me, for He will take of what is Mine and declare it to you. (John 16:13 NKJV)

The Holy Spirit Himself will expose lies and deception. He will guide you into truth. He will lead you on a path through the obstacles the enemy places in your way because He will show you the strategy of the enemy through prayer. He will also show you the Lord's plan in your life.

Dear heavenly Father,

Thank You so very much for the gift of the Holy Spirit. Guide me into Your truth and expose the lies and deception the enemy may have laid in my life. I choose to walk in obedience to Your spirit. Teach me Your ways and give me a deeper understanding of Your love.

In Jesus's name.
Amen.

SPIRIT OF ADDICTIONS

I had a dream. I was in the bathroom on my hands and knees with a toothbrush cleaning the floor. (Interpretation: The bathroom represents repentance. On my knees is a submitted posture in prayer, and the toothbrush has to do with teeth/wisdom, i.e., cleaning up wisdom.) I had been seeking the wisdom of the Lord. I wanted to know Him better; I wanted to be like Enoch was and Moses—a friend of God.

The same night I had the dream of the toothbrush, my friend had a dream that went with mine. In her dream, she saw a mountain and large rocks. Then, she saw the lava running off the mountain and filling the crevices. (Interpretation: The Lord will take you to the mountain and lead you to a hard place in your life—the rock. If you are willing to look at this hard place in your life, then the Holy Ghost fire will pour out of the mountain of heaven and fill every crevice in your life.)

What does it look like to be between a rock and a hard place in our lives? It can look like anything that hinders your relationship with the Lord, including addiction. Some of us do not recognize what exactly an addiction is. Here is a list of some of its manifestations:

1. When someone brings up the issue, you avoid it
2. There is no peace; instead, you feel torment
3. Your finances are drained, and you will even ask for more
4. Division, misunderstandings, and arguments fill your days
5. You are drawn to others with the same addiction (like spirits are drawn to each other)

Addictions run in bloodlines. Sins of the Father shall be visited upon the third and fourth generations. A common saying is, What the parents walk in, the children will run with.' Examine your bloodline, do you see a repeated pattern?

Addiction can develop if you were not properly nurtured as a child. The adult tries to pacify the hole in the heart. Addictions can develop through a trauma in a person's life to subdue the pain. There are many ways addiction can enter an individual's life.

Addictions involve the mind, will, and emotions (soul realm). Addiction is a spirit that is under another spirit by the name of Bondage or Death and is closely associated with the seducing spirit, Python, and familiar spirit. Oh yes, look for the spirit of Whoredoms as well. When we do not deal with the addiction, it can become an idol.

A few days later, I had another dream. I was back in the bathroom. This time, I was looking at the padded toilet lid, and part of the vinyl was torn off. (Interpretation: The Lord wants us to peel back the covering and examine the inside. Dare to look at your hard place/rock and let Him deliver you.)

Tag-Team Spirits

I had to laugh when I discovered spirits like to torment each other. We were in a deliverance years ago when I was commanding a spirit to come out, and he started to negotiate with me. (When that starts, you know you have them right where you want them.) This spirit offered to give up the names of all the other spirits who were residing with him if he could stay. I have learned that the spirits do not like each other, enjoy tormenting each other, and they will not hesitate to throw each other under the bus.

Another time, we were doing several deliverances at once. There were four groups operating in my living room. In one group, the ministers were dealing with a spirit of anger in a young girl. In the next group, the ministers were dealing with a spirit of fear in another girl. The girl with the spirit of anger locked eyes with the girl with the spirit of fear and began to glare very threateningly. The girl with the spirit of fear tried to crawl over the back of her chair to get away from the girl with the spirit of anger. It was incredible to watch the two spirits react to each other. The spirit of anger intimidated the spirit of fear and caused each girl to act accordingly.

Another example of a situation involving tag-team spirits was of a husband and wife who came to us for help. The husband came from a very well-known criminal bloodline, in which twenty-five family members had been killed at different times. And the wife came from a victim bloodline in which her family members turned out to be victims of violent crimes. Are you beginning to see how these spirits tag-team to set people up for failure in life?

It is just like going to a bar, and a man walks in with a seducing spirit, and across the room he locks eyes with a woman with a seducing spirit. The two seducing spirits will draw the two individuals together like a magnet. The foul spirits do not like each other. But they will form alliances to fulfill their evil mission. The spirits that I see teaming up in this season especially against ministries are Leviathan, Python, and Jezebel. I have already written about Leviathan and Python. There is already an excellent book written about the Jezebel spirit, entitled, "Unmasking the Jezebel Spirit" by John Paul Jackson.

PART II

UNDERSTANDING WEAPONS, LEGAL RIGHTS, AND AUTHORITY IN THE SPIRIT

CHAPTER 4

WEAPONS IN WAR

Armor of the Lord (Eph 6:10-18)

HELMET OF SALVATION

We must have the mind of Christ. We need to guard our thoughts and meditate on the good things of the Lord by singing songs to Him, talking to Him, reading the Word and digesting it, acting on what the Word teaches us. We absolutely must renew our mind through the Word. Our brain has little grooves in it where we are conditioned to act or react to stimuli. To change the grooves that our brain creates, we must fill it with the teachings of the Lord to set a new mental groove. We need to reroute our train of thought. By taking captive every "vain imagination" that tries to enter our mind and casting it down, not giving in to it, we create a type of helmet around our thought processes that protects us from the enemy.

The other aspect of this piece of armor is that the head also represents our authority in the spirit as well as in the natural world. When we examine this piece of armor, we must look at our authority. Is our authority submitted to the Lord? Do we walk in a Godly authority? Or do we lord our authority over others?

The Bible has a lot to say about Godly authority. In the church, the leaders are held to a higher accountability. In fact, we are admonished not to seek to be a teacher/leader. We need to consider the cost. We are to take a position of leadership with awareness and reverence of the trust the Lord is placing in us by putting us in such a position over His sheep. He paid a high price for them and tremendously loves them.

This piece of armor is both offensive and defensive in that it protects our thoughts as well as promoting thoughts of walking in our authority in the spirit.

BREASTPLATE OF RIGHTEOUSNESS

The breastplate covers and guards the thorax of a person, which is the heart and chest area. So, what is it that guards our heart? Our right standing with the Lord. It protects our innermost being, the part of us that harbors our will and our emotions.

Sometimes, we are hiding things such as hurt and pain in our hearts and are not aware that there are there. The Bible states that we are to "work out our salvation with fear and trembling." We are to self-examine. We should ask the Lord to examine our hearts and to reveal if there is anything hidden so that it can be made manifest and cleaned out, for out of our mouths we speak what is in our innermost being. We will produce what is in our heart. Our desire should be to create the things of God and make manifest the Kingdom of God.

This piece of armor is both offensive and defensive, too, in that it protects our heart and puts us in a right standing to produce the things of the Kingdom of heaven on earth.

GIRDLE OF TRUTH

The belt of truth is like the fulcrum bar on a scale; it is what measures and distinguishes the truth from a lie.

I will clothe him with your robe and fasten your sash around him and hand your authority over to him (Is 22:21 NKJV). When I studied this out, it became apparent to me that the belt of truth is a sign of authority even when it comes to angels.

When preparing for action, the Hebrews would gird their loins. That means they would pull the skirt of their garment up between their legs and tie it into their belt. Doing so made it easier for them to maneuver in battle. We too must be girded and ready not just physically and mentally but spiritually. We are to be prepared in our authority, standing on the truth of the Word of God.

The belt of truth and the breastplate of righteousness are connected. We have authority given to us through Christ Jesus because of our righteousness (our right standing with Him). It is the belt of truth and the breastplate of righteousness that give us the authority to tread upon all the power of the enemy. Let me say that again—we have authority over the evil cunning and traps of the enemy thanks to the belt of truth, the breastplate of righteousness, and prayer. We must make of our authority a clear righteous stand against the enemy!

This piece of armor is also both offensive and defensive. It is protective in that it provides the ability to distinguish the truth from deception. And it is offensive in that it links with the authority of the helmet and the right standing of the breastplate to enable us to maneuver freely within the the Kingdom of God.

Feet shod with the preparation of the Gospel of Peace

To understand this piece of the armor, we need to break down each aspect of it. Let's look at the feet and what they represent: your path and your direction.

The shoes would speak of your covering as well as your ability to walk that path and direction. One must wear the correct footwear for whatever activity one is doing. For example, if you were to ride a horse, you would want to wear cowboy boots, and if you were to run a race, you would not wear cowboy boots but rather track shoes. Therefore, to carry the gospel of the Kingdom of God, you must walk in the "shoes" of peace, which is a manifestation of the Kingdom of God. Wearing the correct footwear, that of peace, is the ultimate act of trusting the Lord in all things, no matter what comes at you. This covering protects and enhances your ability to carry out your mission.

The Word states that we are to be prepared in season and out of season, always ready to give the good news of our salvation in Christ Jesus. It is through His shedding of blood on the cross at Calvary that we are no longer separated from but are now reconciled to the Lord. Through Christ Jesus, we are brought into a position of peace with the Father in heaven and have access to the Kingdom of God.

There is another aspect of this armor to consider as well, and that is the timing of it.

> And how shall they preach, except they be sent? as it is written, How beautiful are the feet of them that preach the gospel of peace, and bring glad tidings of good things. (Rom. 10:15 KJV)

As we have learned, the word *beautiful* in the Greek means "timely." The good news we carry is readily available and operable in the right timing. Therefore, be ready in season and out of season with the Good News of the Kingdom of God and our salvation through Jesus Christ. Be confident that the Lord has all things in His timing and control, and it is He who directs your path.

SHIELD OF FAITH

Faith is a door. Eph 6:16 says that "Above all, taking the shield[29] of faith, wherewith ye shall be able to quench all the fiery darts of the wicked" (KJV). The word *shield* means "door–like." That means faith opens doors.

One day, I was in the Walmart parking lot getting ready to go inside when my cell phone rang. The female voice on the other end was hysterical; I did not recognize it. I finally figured out who it was on the phone. It was my friend, and her husband had just walked out on her; he wanted a divorce. I called her name into the phone and told her I was holding her hand in the spirit. I closed my eyes, and as I did, I saw a door in front of me. I told her, "Hold my hand and come through the door with me."

She hiccupped, "Okay. I opened the door and verbally walked her through. As soon as we closed the door behind us, she went from emotionally hanging off the ceiling to being like someone had tranquilized her. There was total silence on the phone.

I softly asked, "What happened?"

She said, "I am standing in a green meadow on a hill, and there are flowers all around me. This place where I am standing is so peaceful."

All I could say was "Wow!" The Holy Spirit had led us through the door of faith. The fruit of it was peace!

SWORD OF THE SPIRIT

Revelations 19 tells us the sword comes out of the mouth of the Lord. The sword of the spirit is the Word of God. Jesus spoke the Word of God. In fact, in the desert, during his time of temptation by the enemy, Jesus used the Word against the enemy. We are to speak the word of God. In deliverance, demons will argue with you;

however, when you quote the Word of God, there is no argument. Please read the section in this book on the power of the tongue.

Other Weapons

1. The name of Jesus. At the name of Jesus every knee must bow and every tongue confess He is Lord! Jesus delegated His authority to us. So when we use His name, we are speaking in His character, power, and authority.
2. Anointing oil. I like to use pure oils as these are the life-blood of the plant. Scientists have proven oil has a frequency and the frequency will rise when prayed over. I am particular as to what oil I use depending on what is needed.
3. Blood of Jesus. The blood of Jesus is extremely powerful in deliverance for many reasons. Have you wondered why God required blood in sacrifices? Let me show you something: God breathed into Adam. Blood carries oxygen in the bloodstream. Therefore, when God breathed into Adam, Adam's blood carried the breath of God in his bloodstream. Because God breathed into Adam the breath of life, Adam could not die. Now I understand what the Lord means when He says, "The blood is the life of the animal." It wasn't until sin entered the picture that God pronounced a curse. Rom 6:23 says that "The wages of sin is death" (KJV). Sin polluted the blood.

   Adam broke a spiritual law when he acted on temptation, and this action allowed sin to pierce the veil between heaven and earth. Now sin was in the physical world as well as the spiritual world. Remember, sin brings death.

   Gen 3:21 tells us that it is God Himself, in His love for man, who offered the first sacrifice. When he clothed Adam and Eve, he covered their sin. Those skins, I believe, were not tanned as they are today—they still had the blood on them. The Lord covered their sins with the blood of an animal. He knew Satan is the accuser of the brethren, and he would quickly be in the throne room demanding that the wages of Adam's sin be carried out. The only thing that would cover the sin and satisfy the law that was broken by Adam was blood, because blood contains life and can therefore cover death. That is what the word *atonement* means, "cover."

Let me tell you something else. Demons understand the supernatural power of the blood. In a deliverance, they will sometimes try to scratch or draw blood; this will empower them for a short period of time.

There is also a natural power in blood, researchers at the University of British Colombia in Vancouver have created a battery that can draw power from human blood."[30]- It is is called "a cyborg battery.

On November 5, 2006, The History Channel aired a documentary on "vampirism." This program validated those people who live on blood. Their eyes become weak, and they lose their pigmentation. They also become allergic to the sun. Blood could be a food source for us except for the fact that God has forbidden the eating/drinking of blood. Those who do this are under the same curse as Adam, for they too break the spiritual law of obedience.

Blood has an intoxicating effect. An ancient Aztec tribe that drank blood experienced a euphoric feeling of exhilaration. Blood has healing properties in it. Satanists are well aware of this fact, to the point that they take blood baths to expedite healing and also to slow down the aging process. If the blood of animals and humans can do all of the above, just think what the blood of Jesus can do!

A fetus does not get blood from the mother; it comes from the father. The blood is in the semen. With that in mind, we can understand that Jesus's blood was not of this earth, but from heaven. It was the Holy Spirit who covered Mary to cause her to conceive Jesus; therefore, his blood was pure and not defiled by sin.

Jesus's blood contained:

a. Life. He could not die. He had to "give up the Ghost" on the cross. Man could not kill Him.
b. Redemption/Atonement. Jesus paid the price with His own innocent, pure blood. He was the ultimate trap to the enemy. He was God-breathed and without sin. Therefore, when Satan crucified Him, Satan broke a spiritual law, and this allowed Jesus to take back the keys to the Kingdom of God and give them back to man. Man has dominion. We are now in authority. When Jesus hung on the cross, and his blood dripped down onto the dust below, He uttered those beautiful words, "Forgive them, they know not what they do," His blood contained the spoken words of forgiveness, which covered the dust. God had created man from the dust of the earth. The phrase and the blood covered man on the cross as well as creation.
c. Healing. I Pet 2:24 says, "By His stripes we were healed" (KJV). Remember, there are healing properties in blood.

Jesus's blood does:

a. Cleanses from unrighteousness 1 John 1:7 says that the blood of Jesus puts us in right standing with the Father in heaven.

b. Seals the covenant. There is nothing stronger than a blood covenant. Jesus ushered in the New Covenant of which we are now partakers. "I will put my laws on their hearts" (Heb 10:16-23).

c. Allows us into the presence of God. According to Heb 10:16-23 even into: "The Holy of Holies."

4. The Holy Spirit

When I was a girl, Mom would drop my brother and me off at church on Sunday mornings. The church was across the street from a Pentecostal church. Ross and I would wait and watch as Mom drove around the corner and then run across the street to the Pentecostal church. In our little minds, our church was boring. We didn't want to go to the boring church. The Pentecostal church was not boring. They danced. Ross and I would run across the street, go to that church, and run back across the street in time for Mom to pick us up.

Even at that young age, we knew there was more to this church thing. There is more after salvation. Once you get saved, that is just the beginning. You have invited the Lord into your life, and now that's when things can really happen for you. When you have an encounter with the Holy Spirit, you will know it. You don't have to think, well…I *think* I have. It is a definite date stamped in your mind. Your encounter with the Holy Spirit will light you up spiritually. It is as if you have come out of a sleep, and suddenly you can see and perceive things of the spirit that were previously hidden or confusing to you. Acts 13:52 says,: "And the disciples were filled with joy and with the Holy Spirit" (KJV).

There is an awakening to a depth of love you have never experienced before. Some people say colors seem to be deeper and more vibrant, and you want everyone around you to experience and feel this incredible joy and love. Rom 5:5 says, "And hope maketh not ashamed; because the love of God is shed abroad in our hearts by the Holy Ghost, which is given unto us" (KJV).

Do you remember when you first met the love of your life? Was that person all you wanted to talk about? That is what it is like when you meet the Holy Spirit; you can't help yourself. You want to talk about Him and tell others about His incredible love. The person standing next to you in the grocery line is in for it, let me tell you! Peter experienced this boldness when he spoke to the leaders in Acts 4:8: "Then Peter, filled with the Holy Ghost, said to them, Ye rulers of the people, and elders of Israel" (KJV). Now, this is the same guy who ran from a woman at a campfire when asked about his affiliation with Jesus. After the baptism of the Holy Spirit here he is in Acts 4:8, talking to the rulers and elders of Israel! The Holy Spirit empowers and gives you a boldness to carry out your God-given assignment on earth. Acts 4:31 says, "And when they had prayed the place was shaken where they were assembled together; and they were all filled with the Holy Ghost, and they spake the word of God with Boldness" (KJV).

The gift of the Holy Spirit with the manifestation of tongues is a reversal of the curse that God put on mankind at the tower of Babel in Gen 11:1-9, when God confounded the speech of the people because they were misusing their unity for sinful purposes. In the New Testament, in Acts, the gift of tongues gave people the ability to become truly unified again as they praised the Lord together. That's the proper sense of unity. So, through the cross and under grace, the curse (disunity) was reversed, and a blessing (unity) was brought forward. It is no wonder the gift of tongues is fought so severely. Part of the confusion regarding the gift of tongues has to do with there being four different manifestations of tongues.

> And there appeared unto them cloven tongues like as of fire, and it sat upon each of them. And they were all filled with the Holy Ghost and began to speak with other tongues, as the Spirit gave them utterance (Acts 2:4, KJV),

I remember when I was introduced to the Holy Spirit. I was eight years old, we were at my papa's church, and all the kids were down at the altar seeking the baptism of the Holy Spirit. I was there praying as well when I felt my body start to vibrate. I could hear a lady praying with me in agreement for the baptism. As I was vibrating, she said, "Let go, girl, allow the Holy Spirit to come." I did not understand what "let go" meant. I could hear sounds in my head, but I would not say them; they did not make sense. I eventually started to say the sounds I kept hearing inside of me and noted as I uttered them that they actually fit together. I remember being surprised. It was an incredible experience.

But then, something else happened that night. When I went to bed, I encountered the opposite. An unclean spirit came into my bedroom and sat on my bed. I know now what happened. When I was baptized in the Holy Spirit, I became spiritually aware. Before I was spiritually awakened, I could not see or sense the spiritual realm. But once the Holy Spirit came to me in power, I became aware of both sides of the spiritual coin. The Holy Spirit is your teacher, and the teaching begins immediately.

> But the Comforter, which is the Holy Ghost, whom the Father will send in my name, he shall teach you all things, and bring all things to remembrance, whatsoever I have said to you (John 14:26, NKV).

The Lord loves us. We are God's gift to Jesus. A father's gift to his son. Jesus said, "I have not lost one that you gave me except the son of perdition" (John 17:12 KJV).

Do you realize that Jesus himself staked everything He loved on the Holy Spirit. He left His greatest treasure, His followers, in the keeping, care, and power of the Holy Spirit. With Jesus in the throne room interceding and the Holy Spirit interceding and making supplication within us, how can we fail? There is no way. Two parts of the trinity are interceding. The Holy Spirit prays through us with groanings that cannot be uttered.

"And he that searcheth the heart knows what is in the mind of God" (Rom 8:27 KJV). When we don't know the will of God, what do we do? We are to wait upon the Holy Spirit, and He will make intercession for us. We can have the mind of Christ through the Holy Spirit. He intercedes, knowing the will of God. The Father has a perfect will, and the Holy Spirit lines us up with that will. He will only do this when you get to the place where you give up your will. Your will can get between you and God. When you pray in the spirit, the Holy Spirit will line your will up with the will of the Father. According to the Word, when we pray the Father's will, things happen.

Jesus had to come to a place of laying down His will. He was in the garden of Gethsemane asking the Father to take the cup from him when he laid it down: "Nevertheless, not my will but thy will be done" (Luke 22:42, ESV). Jesus is our example; He is the template we should use when we don't know what to do. He went away from the clutter and noise, separated himself, and prayed. He waited (tarried), and only then was he able to say those wonderful words just quoted.

We are in times now where it is imperative that we know the voice of God and His will. His spirit will bear witness with our spirit … He is the Spirit of truth, and He will keep you from the deception that has come upon the earth.

5. Angels

Angels are mentioned nearly three hundred times in the Bible. There are five different kinds of angels: Seraphs, Cherubim, Arch-angels, Living Creatures, and Angels. The term *angel* means "messenger."

I had encounter with what I perceived to be an angel. When I was the leader of the Glory Riders, which was an equine mounted ministry team that traveled across the United States performing in different venues, uplifting the name of the Lord. This particular year had been intense; we had traveled and worked hard in the ministry for the Lord. We were at our last event for that year, the Veterans Parade in Fresno, Ca. I was walking beside the white horses, as I usually did in a parade. My job was to troubleshoot, make sure little children did not run out in front of a horse or a rider did not get into trouble if a horse spooked at something. I remember talking to the Lord as I walked: "Please get me through this last event…" It had been a very busy year, and I was tired.

The team turned a street corner; I looked down the street and saw that both sides were packed with people. But there was a man who stood out to me; it seemed like all others faded into the background. He was an older African-American man dressed in military fatigues—he looked homeless. He watched the white horses dressed in breast collars declaring "Jesus is Lord" and "Army of the Lord." The riders were flying scarlet flags with the various names of Jesus scrolled across them in gold. I watched him as the team of white horses passed in front of him. He held his hand in the air and praised the Lord. Drawn to him, I walked up smiled and said, "Hello." He glanced at me and continued to praise the Lord. I started to walk on.

It was at that moment that he fastened his intense, intelligent eyes on me and said, "Good job, Carolyn." I was stunned … surely I hadn't heard that right.

I jogged on to keep up with my team. The rider who was riding on the end horse asked me, "Did you know him?"

I said, "No." She had heard him say the same thing.

The Lord knew I was on my last leg. It was the end of a long hard season traveling with the team, and I was so very tired. In His graciousness and love for me, He sent an angel to say, "Good job, Carolyn." I still tear up when I think about that incident.

We have worked with angels in deliverance. My mother and I were in a deliverance with a man who had a severe back issue and was unable to work. During the deliverance, my mom saw an angel standing behind the man; I did not see it. Mom told the man about the angel standing behind him. At about the time she finished saying that statement, the six-foot-four man was lifted up completely off the chair and floor. We all heard his back snap, crackle, and pop. He was totally fine and could walk!

How do I know if an angel is good or bad? Once again, know them by their fruits: Matt 7:15-20. Try the spirit. Three times I have had angels come to me and I tried them as the Bible instructs us to do. I asked them, "Are you from Jesus, who died, rose again, and sits at the Father's right side?" One disappeared, one was sucked into the wall, and one blew up!

CHAPTER 5

SPIRITUAL COVERINGS

IN THE CHURCH

A good healthy church works like a well-oiled machine with all the gifts, offices and various activities of the spirit in working order. Each person is giving and submitting to each other's office and gifts.

Someone once explained to me the positions in the church this way. Look at your hand; each digit on your hand represents a spiritual office. The thumb is the apostle, as the thumb can touch all of the other fingers/offices. The pointer finger is the prophet, as the prophet points the direction. The middle finger is the tallest and represents the evangelist, as he is the one who goes out into the byways and highways to minister. The ring finger is the pastor, as he is in love with the Lord's flock. The little finger is the teacher, because when you form a fist and rest it on a table, it is on the teacher that everything rests.

A covering in a church is the body of Christ fitted jointly together, praying for each other and ministering to one another. Eph. 5:21 mentions "submitting to one another in the fear of God" (NKJV).

I do not believe in "lone wolves" in the sheep's pen—a person who is unwilling to submit to authority. If you are a person who turns tail the minute you hear something from the pulpit you do not agree with, then you are setting yourself up for failure. It is easy to say you will submit in the Body of Christ only until something happens you do not like or something is said that offends you. We must become submitted to each other, willing to accept sound teachings as well as discipline. The Bible exhorts us to "Obey those who rule over you, and be submissive, for they watch out for your souls, as those who must give account. Let them do so with joy and not with grief, for that would be unprofitable for you" (Heb. 13:17 NKJV).

We are to submit to those the Lord puts in authority as leaders within the church, as God holds them to a higher accountability because of their position. The Bible encourages us not to make their job more difficult. When we come against these men and women of God in their office, we are coming against the Lord.

A Godly leader is appointed by the Lord to teach, encourage, and exhort, which means, according to the *Strong's Concordance*, "To call near" their flock. They are not there to control you but to help you learn how to grow and operate in the Kingdom of God. You need to understand that there are spiritual laws and ways of doing things and that we don't just come into the body of Christ already knowing them.

> And we urge you, brethren, to recognize those who
> labor among you, and are over you in the Lord and
> admonish you, and to esteem them very highly in love
> for their work's sake. Be at peace among yourselves.
> Now we exhort you, brethren, warn those who are
> unruly, comfort the fainthearted, uphold the weak,
> be patient with all. (1 Th. 5:12-14, NKJV)

One of the responsibilities of a church leader is to monitor who is allowed behind the pulpit. I have seen some horrible things happen due to negligence in guarding the pulpit. Delegated spiritual authority is granted to an individual who is allowed to stand behind the podium, whether it is temporarily or permanently. If an evil spirit has authority, it can move like wildfire throughout the congregation. It is the church leadership's responsibility to ensure the well-being of the flock by monitoring who is allowed to speak from the pulpit.

With all of that said, there is a shift going on right now in the body of Christ. I believe the Lord is leading us into more of an apostolic movement. What does that mean? It means the Lord is looking for "a full-grown Bride for His return, not a little girl," to quote from my friend Donna Huffman.

We are to develop our intimacy with the Holy Spirit. We are to learn to hear and be taught by Him.

> But the anointing which you have received from Him abides in you, and you do not need that anyone teach you; but as the same anointing teaches you concerning all things, and is true, and is not a lie, and just as it has taught you, you will abide in Him. (1 John 2:27, NKJV).

So the question arises, how do we reconcile these two ideas, to submit both to leadership and to the Holy Spirit? The Holy Spirit is not going to teach another gospel. In other words, the church leaders should hear from the same spirit as you do—none other than the Holy Spirit. He will not tell the leadership one thing and you another. He may show the leadership more than what He is telling you regarding the church government.

What if what the leaders are hearing is different from what I am hearing? If that is the case, pray; do not go around the church talking to others about it. In all actuality, if you do that, you are trying to get others to side with you on the matter. Ask to speak with the leadership and talk about the issue. If that does not resolve the situation, sit and wait upon the Holy Spirit. The immaturity of the believer is the thought pattern that goes, "If I do not agree with this or that, then I will just leave." That is an immature mindset, and you will find yourself in a revolving door.

So in conclusion, submit one to another in love; try not to make the church leader's job more difficult than it already is. Understand the Lord appoints leaders in their office and works alongside of them. Hear from the Holy Spirit as to what your position is in the church. Be willing to take your position in the body of Christ, so that it may work as God intended.

In the Workplace

The person in authority opens and closes doors.

When you place yourself in a working environment and agree to the terms of that particular workplace, you come into a covenant with their belief system. You enter into agreement with whatever spiritual authority is at the top. What that can do is open you up for either blessings or foul visitation(s).

Now, I do not want you to go run and quit your job because I said so. I am just making you aware of possibilities for blessings to be tapped into or for you to be able to block enemy access into your home. And remember, you have spiritual authority as well. The Bible states that wherever you place your foot you take the Kingdom of God. The Lord may have called you to your employment to do just that.

Have you ever noticed that if someone in the workplace gets a divorce, it seems to sweep through the office? Pretty soon Sally is having marital problems, and then Jane, and so on.

My husband started working for a man who was having marital problems and was getting a divorce. We began to have the same issues within ten months of his employment. The man my husband was working for was in fear and became a workaholic. This man claimed to be a Christian and probably was, but his motivation in the company was fear. He had an enormous overhead and lifestyle, which put incredible pressure on him. As a result, his home life suffered and the very thing he was trying to protect he lost.

As another example, we were in a deliverance with a gentleman who was having high blood pressure and heart problems. After a bit of delving into his work environment, we found he had started a new job about a year before. We asked when these physical symptoms started. "About a year ago" was the answer. Well, it did not take a genius to put two and two together and realize there was a connection. Through more questioning, we discovered that his boss was full of fear and insecurity. Boom—there it was; he had placed himself under this man's authority, and the spirit of fear/anxiety had come upon him. So when we enter into covenant with someone over us in authority, who operates in fear, we need to guard our relationships. Again, I am pointing out possible enemy access.

On the flip side, if you place yourself under an authority who operates in the Kingdom of God, putting the Lord first, those blessings of the "cup overflowing" will flow upon you as well. I once worked for a gentleman who was a Christian and followed Godly principles. This man made a huge amount of money every year; therefore, as he prospered, so did my business. His overflow got on me.

To sum this all up, be aware of the human authority you place yourself under, as you may take on their issues and blessings. As employees, we come into agreement with the spiritual authorities as well. But remember, you have spiritual authority and take the Kingdom of God wherever you go. Do not be afraid; just be wise. The Word states, "Wise as a serpent, soft as a dove." You are the ultimate covering over your spirit and home.

IN THE FAMILY

I want to talk about the parable of marriage. Those of you who are married, did you know you are a living a parable? Everything about marriage is a graphic illustration of how the Lord feels about His church. In fact, according to John and Lisa Bevere's teaching in "The Story of Marriage," marriage is the image of God.

> So God created man in His image; in the image of God He created him; male and female He created them (Gen. 1:27, NKJV).

Have you ever noticed that scripture tells the husband to love his wife and tells the wife to respect the husband. Why do you suppose He commanded the husband to love? Do you suppose it was because the Lord knew that was going to be an area that men would need to work on? Love is a choice, not just a feeling.

And what about women, who are commanded to respect our husbands? Do you think that may be due to the fact respect is an issue for a female? The instruction for husbands to love their wives and wives to respect their husbands are not suggestions, they are commands. We need to ensure that we take every step possible to be obedient to these commands. We need to remember to honor each other in this endeavor.

It is one thing to be married; it is quite another for a couple to "be mated" in the spirit. To be mated is a supernatural welding that happens between two people when they are united in Christ. By nature, it implies unity—becoming one—which illustrates the relationship of God with His people. The groom is to love his bride as Jesus loved the church and died for her. It is the husband's job to protect his wife, not just from outside attacks but even from himself. It is his job to offer her security in her mind and heart. Remember,

Eve was taken from a bone out of Adam's rib. That represents the fact that she came from under his arm. She is to be able to stand under the protection of her husband's arm.

My husband went through a period when the Lord was speaking to him about nurturing our marriage. This conversation between him and the Lord went on for several months; the Lord would drop words into his spirit, and he would learn to use what the Lord showed him.

Here is a list of what the Lord showed him:

1. We can do this
2. Come with me
3. Let's talk
4. Let's pray
5. We have more going for us than the enemy has going against us.
6. I love my wife
7. Let's ride
8. Protect my wife
9. The buck stops here
10. Don't turn this car around

Men, in this parable of marriage, you represent the Father in heaven. How would He treat His bride? You are to act, speak, and behave accordingly. Is the Father abusive? No! Is he impatient? No! The Lord operates in "love, joy, peace, longsuffering, gentleness, goodness, faith, meekness, temperance" (Gal. 5:22-23 KJV). Col. 3:19 says, "Husbands, love your wives, and be not bitter against them" (NKJV). Men, you set the tone in your house. If you don't like it, change it. One might try to make the statement, "Carolyn, He is God, I am human with faults…" Let me tell you, He too has emotions and feels.

Ex. 34:14 says, "For thou shalt worship no other god: for the LORD, whose name is Jealous, is a jealous God" (KJV). Just like any other person, should his mate (the bride) commit adultery, He is jealous. So how do we commit adultery? We commit adultery by whoring with the world—doing and saying things we know better than to do or say.

1 Cor. 7:4 says, "The wife hath not power of her body, but the husband: and likewise also the husband hath not power of his own body, but the wife" (KJV). Men, you belong to the Lord. Once you were saved and baptized into Christ, according to Galatians, you put on Christ. Your actions and everything else are now His. Your sins, Jesus paid for; you no longer own them, they are His, covered in His blood. He redeemed you; he paid for you at a dear price. You are now the temple of the most high God.

The Lord will defend His bride. Is. 35:4 tells us, "Say to them that are of a fearful heart, Be strong, fear not: behold, your God will come with vengeance, even God with a recompense; he will come and save you" (KJV). The Lord loves His bride; He is protective and jealous of her. You, as a believer, are His bride!

Eph. 5:25-26 says, "Husbands, love your wives, even as Christ also loved the church, and gave himself for it; That he might sanctify and cleanse it with the washing of water by the word" (NKJV).

Husbands, your prayers cover your home. You have supernatural authority over that home. You are accountable for the stewardship/ management of your home and relationships in that home. The blessings flow from Father in heaven to Jesus to husband to wife. If the household is out of order, then there is a squeeze in the pipeline of blessings.

Men, did you know that your prayers can be hindered due to not honoring your wife? To honor means "to esteem as valuable."

> Likewise, ye husbands, dwell with them according to knowledge, giving honor unto the wife, as unto the weaker vessel, and as being heirs together of the grace of life; that your prayers be not hindered. (1 Pet. 3:7, KJV)

We are joint heirs together. We are one flesh and made in the image of God.

> So ought men to love their wives as their bodies. He that loveth his wife loveth himself. For no man ever yet hated his own flesh; but nourisheth and cherisheth it, even as the Lord the church: For we are members of his body, of his flesh, and of his bones. For this cause shall a man leave his father and mother, and shall be joined unto his wife, and they two shall be one flesh (Eph. 5:28-31 KJV).

A husband and wife are one flesh. We have found that if one of the spouses holds unforgiveness, it can affect the other physically in a negative way. (See the chapter on unforgiveness.)

Now here is another aspect of this relationship between the men and the Father in heaven. You have to take the female role and allow Him to protect you, cherish you, love you, and nurture you. As you would like your wife to be, so should you be with Father. Is. 54:5 says, "For thy Maker is thine husband; the LORD of hosts is his name, and thy Redeemer the Holy One of Israel; The God of the whole earth shall he be called" (KJV).

Let's see, what would that look like: honoring the mate, attentive, passionate in the relationship, protective, and so on. Pr 31:11 tells us, "The heart of her husband doth safely trust in her, so that he shall have no need of spoil" (KJV).

Again, it is all about unity—becoming one—in the marriage, working toward that goal. This is the parable and illustrates the relationship of God with His people. The groom is to love his bride as Jesus loves the church and died for her. The bride is to honor and respect the groom as the church regards God.

To steward marriage by maintaining honor and love in the relationship is to position oneself for an increase of favor with God and man. It is when this relationship is held in proper esteem that the message of God's love is most clearly seen in this world.

Over the Children

In the previous section on marriage, we saw that the hierarchy of blessings for the family flows from the Father in heaven to Jesus to the husband, then to the wife, and then to the children.

A Godly husband is in close relationship with the Lord through the Holy Spirit. The Holy Spirit will guide and show him how to train up his children in the way that they should go, according to their individual personality types. It is the husband in the house that has ultimate accountability and stewardship in answering to the Lord.

> Or if a woman makes a vow to the LORD, and binds herself by some agreement while in her father's house in her youth, and her father hears her vow and the agreement by which she has bound herself, and her father holds his peace, and then all her vows shall stand, and every agreement with which she has bound herself shall stand. But if her father overrules her on the day that he hears, then none of her vows nor her agreements by which she has bound herself

shall stand; and the LORD will release her because her father overruled her. (Num. 30:3-5, NKJV)

There is a supernatural authority the husband is given to carry out his role as head of household. In fact, when it comes to doing deliverance on a child, it is vital that the spiritual covering be in agreement with it.

The Lord will partner with him to ensure the safety and wellbeing of his home. Let me give you an example. I know of a couple who had an eighteen-year-old daughter. She decided to run away with a young man whom the parents did not approve of for some obvious reasons. The more involved in the relationship with him she became, the more rebellious she was to parental authority and those who were trying to protect her.

The mother and daughter were having issues in their relationship. One day, the mother asked her if she would like to spend a few days with her aunt and uncle to take a "breather." She quickly responded, "Yes." While she was visiting with them, she made arrangements with this young man to sneak away. As she was sneaking out of the house, her uncle caught her in the truck, and the young man tried to run him over; the two young people got away.

While this was going on, the parents were in town doing errands. The cell phone rang in the car and the wife answered it. It was her sister; she informed her that her daughter had run away with the young man. She went on to say that she and her husband were on their way to the mother's house.

The father and mother sped home, frantically trying to figure out what to do. When they got there, the sister and her husband arrived and started to plan on how to get the wayward girl home safely. The father took his rightful position as his daughter's spiritual covering and announced that the family was to go after her; plans were put into motion to initiate a strategic intervention.

The parents contacted their daughter's best friend and enlisted her help in maneuvering the daughter out of the boy's house; the friend agreed to join them in this endeavor. The parents then contacted another individual, whom the teenage girl respected, and then contacted this person's son, who was a marine stationed near where she'd run off to. The father was a pilot and made arrangements to get plane to fly part of the group to where the girl was. You have to envision what all this looked like. Here they were going after her from the North in the air and on land, as well as having a marine coming in from the South to where their daughter was staying. The plan was to get her and take her to some friends in Texas, who had been through a similar situation and were connected with a healthy church.

Before they left the house, the mother heard a little voice in her head telling her to take their daughter's passport. She thought, *Why would I need her passport?* But she obeyed the little voice and put it in her purse. The sister loaded up her car with a couple of friends who were strong in the Lord and were spiritual warriors.

As everyone was walking out of the door of the house to leave, the mother received a phone call from one of the church intercessors. (Understand, no one in church had heard about this.) The intercessor on the phone sobbed, "I had a vision. I saw a black umbrella open and on the handle was blood. Then I saw an enormous white canopy overlay it, and angels rush in!" The mother thanked her, feeling assured that the Lord was going to assist in getting her daughter back. She knew from the vision that the daughter had placed herself under a black covering and that the white canopy that overlaid the situation was the rescue group coming in, assisted by angels.

On the flight down, the father and uncle planned how to carry out the operation. The men strategized and came up with a plan for the daughter's friend to invite her to dinner; then, at the restaurant, the group would get her into one of the vehicles. The mother and friend stayed back at the airport while the others surrounded the restaurant and waited.

The daughter and boyfriend met her friend at the restaurant. The three were seated there when the father walked up to the table. "Dad! What are you doing here?" she asked. The father explained that he wanted to talk to her outside; between her friend and the father, they were able to convince the daughter to go outside and talk. When she got outside, they ushered her into the marine's truck.

In the meantime, the boyfriend realized what had happened and barreled out of the restaurant door, running smack dab into the uncle, who had played linebacker in college football. The kid realized he was face to face with the very man he had previously tried to run down with his car. "Remember me?" asked the uncle. The kid's face turned ashen. He retreated, apparently to call the police to report a kidnapping.

The daughter, safely tucked inside the truck seated between the marine's mother and her aunt, was driven to the airport. Back at the airport, the mother and friend waited. As the truck pulled into the parking lot, the mother opened the door to where her daughter sat. The girl was livid with the mother and voiced it. Her mother told her this was not her doing, but her father's.

Within a few minutes, the marine's mother yelled, "Get in the car! The police are on their way!" The marine jumped in the driver's seat, the parents into the backseat with their daughter safely tucked between them. and the car sped out of the gates of the airport. The group must have looked like fleas scattering as the various vehicles dispersed before the police arrived. Just as they approached the first stop sign, a police car flew around the corner and sped toward the airport. The police car passed so close to the "getaway" truck that the occupants of the truck could look right down into the lap of the police officer. The incredible part was that the officer did not see the truck. I have heard of people smuggling Bibles into different countries and officials not seeing them, but a whole truck? The mother remembered the vision that was told to her earlier that day—angels rushing in.

As everyone drove the freeways trying to decide what to do, they could see the others in their respective cars crisscrossing on freeway interchanges; it looked like something out of a Laurel and Hardy movie. They could all see each other at different times but could not get on the same freeway together. In the chaos, no one thought to use his or her cell phone.

While the getaway chase was in play, the marine parked the truck behind some old buildings so the parents could talk with their daughter and convince her to come home. The mother and daughter got out of the vehicle, the daughter still livid, and mother crying. The mother realized the circumstance was a manifestation of a spiritual curse. She mentally went over the family history: her grandmother had run away, albeit for just a couple of hours; her mother had run away for three days; and now the daughter had run. She stopped in the middle of the conversation and said, "I break this curse right now! You will not feel the pain I am experiencing at this moment!" The daughter looked at her somewhat surprised and nodded her head in agreement. The parents continued to talk with her, but to no avail.

About that time, the marine received a phone call telling him to get back to the airport, that the police wanted to talk to all involved. The mother thought, *Oh gosh, they have our friends.* The parents agreed they needed to return to the airport. The mother turned to the marine and said, "You cannot be connected with us in this situation as it might hurt your career in the military." She could see the battle in his eyes, as he did not want her to be the one who would take the heat from the police. She then turned to her husband and said, "You cannot get arrested either; you are the only one who can fly the airplane home." Having made her point, she then turned back to the marine and said, "I need your keys."

The two men climbed into the backseat, one on either side of the girl, and the mother climbed into the driver's seat. They reluctantly headed back to the airport. As they drove, the mother told the daughter, "We love you so much. We will not allow you to go down this path. If that means I get arrested, then so be it. But know we love you."

As they approached the airport, they stopped short of the entrance, and the father got out of the truck and crawled through a side fence to get to the airplane. It was dark. The mother turned in to the airport entrance and reiterated to her baby girl, "I love you." Taking a deep breath, she sighed, "Here we go."

Sure enough, as they pulled in, headlights snapped on; it was the police car. She stopped the truck, fully expecting to be arrested for kidnapping. Instead, the police car slowly drove past them! What? Again, she looked down into the lap of an officer as he cruised by. The officer did not see them. She was so stunned she sat there a moment, not breathing and having no idea what to do next. Her husband had made it to the airplane and was already spooling up the engines; he and part of the group were headed home.

She made a phone call to find out where everyone was waiting; they were at a nearby restaurant. The marine, daughter, and mother headed to the restaurant. They met the remainder of the group, and the daughter and mother climbed into the car with her aunt. While the uncle and friend jumped in the other car, the group headed to an out-of-state airport to fly to Texas.

They drove for what seemed like hours. It was late and they were exhausted, to say the least. They stopped at a motel in the middle of nowhere; it looked like the Bates Motel in *Psycho*. The uncle checked in at the front desk and came back with the key to their room. He opened the door and immediately disconnected the phone in the room. He then laid a pallet on the floor, blocking the doorway, and that is where he slept for the night.

The next morning, they headed for an international airport. Upon arriving at the airport, they returned the rental car they had been driving. The uncle and friend jumped in his car and headed back home, while the aunt, daughter, and mother headed into the airport. They approached the counter to purchase their tickets and realized the daughter had left her purse back at the boy's house— she had no identification. The Lord was already prepared for this, of course; He had instructed the mother to bring the daughter's passport. They were in the clear. While passing through security checkpoints, the mother was terrified her daughter would scream out for help, but she remained silent.

Upon arrival at the international airport in Texas, the aunt turned on her cell phone only to find several messages waiting. The first was the insurance company informing her that their vehicle was covered for damage in an accident. The second said that her young son had to be taken to the emergency room, as he was terribly ill. And the third informed her that her husband and friend had been in an accident as they left the airport. And he was calling to let her know everyone was alright. The enemy was ticked off and he was fighting back; but the little group knew he had already lost this battle; as the Lord had clearly stated before they had left home, He had sent His angels in to assist.

The mother and daughter stayed a month in Texas, being ministered to by compassionate, loving people. Both the mother and daughter were battle wounded, broken, and in need of healing. But because of a father who took seriously his spiritual position as head of the household, operated in his spiritual authority, and was joined by a wife who fully supported his stance, God stepped in to assist them in getting things back on course.

The daughter is now married to a precious man, whom they dearly love. She sings on the worship team at her church and is thankful for the intervention.

> Children, obey your parents in the Lord, for this is right. Honor your father and mother," which is the first commandment with promise: that it may be well with you and you may live long on the earth. And you, fathers, do not provoke your children to wrath, but bring them up in the training and admonition of the Lord (Eph. 6:1-4, NKJV).

CHAPTER 6

THE POWER OF SPEECH

THE TONGUE

There is power in the spoken word!

> Come, you children, listen to me; I will teach you
> the fear of the LORD. Who is the man who desires
> life, And loves many days, that he may see good?
> Keep your tongue from evil,
> And your lips from speaking deceit. Depart from
> evil and do good;
> Seek peace and pursue it (Ps 34:11-14 NKJV).

In other words, the first area of our life that should manifest the fear of the Lord is in how we talk. If we desire a long and prosperous life, the first thing we must realize is that we need a healthy respect for the Lord. And when we have this honor for our precious Lord, it is reflected in the way we speak and act. Many people will tell me, "I fear the Lord!" Really? Then why are you telling off-color jokes or gossiping? There is a difference between loving the Lord and having a healthy respect for Him.

When I was young, I loved the Lord, but it did not keep me from backsliding. It was not until I understood "the love and fear of the Lord" that I straightened up and flew right. Pr 15:4 says, "A wholesome[31] [medicine/healing]- tongue is a tree of life: but perverseness[32] [distortion/misuse]- therein is a breach[33] [fracture/leak]- in the spirit" (NKJV). In other words, the healing of the tongue is life; but the misuse of it shows a fracture or leak in our spirit. There is a direct link between our mouth and spirit. The way we speak is a surefire gauge to the condition of our heart.

> Either make the tree good and its fruit good, or else make the tree bad and its fruit bad; for a tree is known by its fruit. Brood of vipers! How can you, being evil, speak good things? For out of the abundance of the heart the mouth speaks (Matt. 12:33-34 NKJV).

For out of the abundance of heart/spirit, our mouth speaks. Our words are a direct gauge for where our true walk with God is.

In one of his teachings, Arthur Burk gave a great analogy:

> When we are sick, we go to the doctor, right? What is the first thing the doctor will have you do? He will ask you to stick out your tongue. The doctor can tell a lot about your physical body by the condition of your tongue. The same is in the spirit, if you go for a checkup with the Lord. Do you know the first thing He is going to do? He is going to tell you to stick out your tongue just like a regular doctor. And just like in natural medicine, the tongue will tell the truth whether you are sick or well.

There are many diseases our mouths need to be healed of:

1. Talking too much (Pr 10:19)
2. Idle/careless words (Matt 12:36)
3. Gossip (Lev 19:16)
4. Lying (Pr 6:16-19); lying has a place in the lake of fire (Rev 21:8)
5. Flattery (Prov 26:28)
6. Hastiness of speech (Pr 29:20)

According to the Lord, all of these are sins. The wages of sin is death. There is a penalty to pay if it goes unchecked and unrepentant. If you have roots of resentment, unbelief, impurity or pride, this it will come out in the way you speak. If you are speaking negatively or judgmentally, there needs to be healing. Mentally, stick out your spiritual tongue; what is it saying about your walk with the Lord?

In deliverance, we create weapons to use against the enemy by speaking them into existence. I have lost count of the times we have pulled spiritual weapons out of people from others who have spoken negatively about them.

Now let me show you something else—what you speak will alter your future. In Numbers, the Lord spoke to the Israelites about their complaining in the desert.

> God said, as ye have spoken in mine ears, so will I do to you: your carcasses shall fall in the wilderness …. From twenty years old and upward, which have murmured against me, doubtless ye shall not come into the land. (Nu 14:26 KJV)

Therefore, not only were the men who gave the evil report going to die in the wilderness, so were those who complained. What does that show us? It shows that what we profess out of our mouth we will own. And those who complain will never find that place of rest that God says is available to us.

Jesus gave us an example of how you are talk. David wrote about it in Psalms:.

You are fairer than the sons of men; Grace[34] [favor, quality of kindness] is poured upon Your lips; Therefore God has blessed You forever" (Ps 45:2 NKJV).

One of the signs of the Messiah is in the way He speaks!

> Then the officers came to the chief priests and Pharisees, who said to them, "Why have you not brought Him?" The officers answered, "No man ever spoke like this Man!" (John 7:45-46, NKJV)

If a person has the Holy Spirit within him or her, that person should be speaking with grace (favor).-

The Song of Solomon is written to show the love and intimacy of the Holy Spirit toward His bride (us). Let's see the beautiful description of the Bride of Christ: "Your lips are like a scarlet thread, and your mouth is lovely. Your temples are like a slice of a pomegranate behind your veil" (Song of Solomon 4:3 NAS). The first thing that was pointed out is the mouth. The scarlet thread is a representative of the blood of Jesus. Our lips should be sanctified, covered, and guarded by the blood of Jesus.

> Your lips, my bride, drip honey; honey and milk are under your tongue, and the fragrance of your garments is like the fragrance of Lebanon (Song of Solomon 4:11, NAS).

The promised land was filled with milk and honey. There is covenant in the promised land with the Lord. Your covenant should be set upon your lips. Only good things should come from your mouth. Our garments have the fragrance of Lebanon. The cedars of Lebanon are known for their towering strength. You are strong in the Lord, and you should be declaring such things.

If you tongue needs to be healed, let us pray together:

Our Father in heaven, glory to Your name. I praise You this day and honor You. I thank You for Your son, Jesus Christ, who died for me on the cross to set me free. I thank You for His precious blood that washes me clean.

Lord, I have a confession to make. I need help to control my tongue. I understand that my tongue is speaking what is in my heart. Therefore, Lord, my heart needs to be healed as well.

I ask you, Lord, to forgive me and cleanse me of all these things, my tongue and heart; I ask You to heal them. I repent and ask You to forgive me, Lord. I ask You to put a guard over my mouth and I ask You, Lord, to fill me with the Holy Spirit, in Jesus's name. Amen

LYING

The Lord woke me one morning at 3:11 a.m., so I got out of bed and picked up my Bible and asked him, "Lord, where do I start?" He answered, "Genesis 3." I opened the Bible to see what He wanted to show me, and the verse that jumped out at me was Gen. 3:3: "But of the fruit of the tree which is in the midst of the garden, God has said, 'You shall not eat it, nor shall you touch it, lest you die'" (NKJV).

Wow! Lord, that is the first lie in the Bible. You did not tell Eve not to touch it; you told Adam not to eat it, but someone, Adam or Eve, added to your original command. Do you see the tiny little twist of the truth? That little twist gave access to the enemy to mess with Eve's mind. To believe a lie, no matter what the lie, gives the enemy access to mess with you.

In deliverance, I have found lying to be fear based. In other words, it is the fear of something that causes a person to fib. It can be the fear of man, fear of rejection, fear of consequences…whatever it is, it is still fear. Fear is the opposite of faith. It is by faith that we please God. So, if we are in fear, we cannot please God. If we are dealing with the fear of man, we have put other people's opinions above what the Lord wants: This is a problem.

We must go to the root of the issue that allowed fear to enter. According to Henry Wright, author of the book *A More Excellent Way*, fear is the result of a breach in one of three areas.[35]

1. A broken relationship between you and God
2. A broken relationship between you and another person
3. A broken relationship between you and yourself

According to 1 John 4:18, "Perfect love casts out fear." Once you identify where the break is, the spirit of fear leaves immediately, and you can dislodge the lying spirit as well. Since reading that fear is allowed entrance through broken relationships, I have been able to go right to the root of the problem when dealing with a spirit of fear and easily cast that spirit out.

GOSSIPING: GOSSIP GRENADES

Jesus did not come to nullify the Law of Moses but to fulfill it. In the Old Testament, the people would have to take a perfect animal, an animal without blemish, to the priest as a sacrifice to roll their sins over for another year. This sacrifice did not atone for their sins but pushed them out for another year.

When Jesus died on the cross, giving Himself to atone for our sins, it was the ultimate and perfect sacrifice. Why? Because Jesus's blood came from heaven and contained no error; it was pure and unblemished. His blood carried no generational defilement.

After Jesus had died, He rose from the tomb, entered the temple of heaven, and poured his blood out on that altar. The last sacrifice ever required by the Lord. The Law is fulfilled—Jesus's words while hanging on the cross were, "It is finished."

A bit of a side note: In reading the New Testament, after Jesus sprinkled His blood on the altar of heaven, I do not see Satan entering heaven again. The temple and altar of heaven are clean, and Satan is the defiled one. The only way now for the "accuser of the brethren" to accuse you before the Lord is to use another person or yourself. How is he able to do this? By using your mouth and your actions—by using gossip.

Have you ever noticed when someone begins to gossip about someone else, it can seem like a delicious morsel, how it makes our flesh kind of stand up? *What tantalizing thing am I going to hear?*

In church circles, we often gossip under the guise of "We need to pray for so and so," and then we go on and tell the gory details instead of just leaving it at "we need to pray for so and so." It is a trick of the enemy to get us unknowingly to spread gossip. Some will preface their statement with, "I know I shouldn't say this, but..." That one little word *but* erases everything spoken before it. Still others will use sarcasm. Personally, I detest this. I asked the Lord why does sarcasm feel like fingernails on a chalkboard to me? He said because it is criticism hidden behind humor. To me, sarcasm combined with gossip is a double-edged sword.

There is something lacking in a person's life when they need to put others down or expose their failures. Perfect love casts out fear, and it also covers a multitude of sins, not exposes them. People who are lacking in love are unhappy about themselves or a situation. Such a person is most likely to harbor unforgiveness and/or self-hatred, and it can come out sideways in the form of gossip.

In situations where you are tempted to gossip, even inadvertently, you have to ask yourself, "Do I want to be constructive or destructive? Am I going to tear down or build a bridge?" Remember this, if you have to justify your actions or what you say to make yourself feel better, then your words and/or actions are probably wrong.

Let's look at gossip? What is it? It is the spreading of rumors or idle, fruitless tales.–[36] The apostle Paul described some of the early believers as "not only idle but gossips [tattlers] and busybodies" (1 Tim 5:13 AMP). Jesus stated, "For every idle word men may speak, they will give account of it in the day of judgment" (Matt 12:36 NKJV).

Pr 16:28 says, "A perverse man stirs up dissension, and a gossip separates close friends" (NIV).

Note the linking of two spirits here. Spirits work as a team to bring about destruction. We can see in the previous scriptures that a perverse spirit will link with a haughty spirit (strongman over gossip). I will go into "tag-team" spirits in a later chapter.

Pr 18:8 says, "The words of a talebearer are like wounds, and they go down into the innermost parts of the belly" (KJV). The words of a talebearer are as wounds—"piercing" like a "sword," "they go down into the innermost parts of the belly." The talebearer's story wounds, at once, the person being talked to and the person being talked about, as well as the person doing the talking. Though the hearer may seem to make light of it, the poison goes down deeply, leaving him or her in suspicion, distrust, or dislike.[37]

God created us in His image; and therefore, we, too, create with our mouth. By speaking words against a person, in the spirit, we are stabbing them in the back. We leave a wound and sometimes even a weapon in them. Many times in deliverance or inner healing, we are pulling out spiritual arrows and knives from a person's back. When we delve into the reason that it lodged there, we find that other people have been talking behind their back.

As I have already stated, the person doing the gossiping is affected too. What you speak, you will own. Matt. 7:1 plainly tells us not to judge so that we will not be judged. And in God's Word, the Lord tells us that the measure of mercy we show to others is with the same measure of mercy God will show to us.

Pr 20:19 says, "A gossip betrays a confidence; so avoid a man who talks too much" (NIV). My business partner used to say, "A dog that brings you a bone will take a bone." In other words, a person who brings you a choice morsel of gossip will listen to what you have to say and carry it to the next person. This gossipy person needs help. They bring destruction wherever they go, and their personal life is usually undisciplined, a roller coaster ride.

> These six things the LORD hates, Yes, seven are an abomination to Him: 17 A proud look, A lying tongue, Hands that shed innocent blood, A heart that devises wicked plans, Feet that are swift in running to evil, A false witness who speaks lies, And one who sows discord among brethren. (Pr 6:16-19, NIV)

So what is a gossip linked to?

1. Lacks judgment
2. Betrays a confidence
3. Separates friends
4. Stirs up dissension
5. Wounds the hearer as well as the victim

Ultimately, the Lord considers gossip worse than most other sins we consider vile. Because when we verbalize such things, we are putting ourselves in judgment against another person; and according to the Bible, when we judge another, that same judgment is upon us. No wonder we find ourselves in bondage.

The proper way to release frustration is to choose mercy, compassion, and understanding. Take time to look at the situation from the other person's perspective.

So all this being said, what are we going to do about it? We have to recognize it for what it is—gossip. A person who is wanting to gossip will come at you like someone with a hand grenade; if you let them pull the pin it doesn't matter who is holding the grenade—you both will get it!

So when you see someone coming at you with a gossip grenade, you immediately stop that person from pulling the pin. Tell them, "I don't want to hear it!" Then run. They may still pull it, and you need to be out of the blast radius. As the Word clearly states, avoid the very appearance of evil.

GRUMBLING

> Neither murmur ye, as some of them also murmured, and were destroyed of the destroyer. (I Cor. 10:10, KJV)

Who is this destroyer? Rev. 9:11 tells us, "And they had a king over them, which is the angel of the bottomless pit, whose name in the Hebrew tongue is Abaddon, [Destroyer] but in the Greek tongue hath his name Apollyon" (KJV).

We see from this scripture, Destroyer is a prince, a ruling principle, over the bottomless pit. Note that he is also a fallen angel. According to the word, one angel can kill one hundred thousand men. These angels have great strength and, being that he is a ruler over the bottomless pit, he also has an army to back him up.

The definition of *Abaddon* (Hebrew word) according to the Catholic Encyclopedia is: "ruin, destruction (Job 31:12), place of destruction; the abyss, realm of the dead (Job 26:6; Pr 15:11). It occurs personified, as well, in Apocalypse 9:11 as Abaddon and is rendered in Greek by Apollyon, denoting the angel-prince of hell, the minister of death, and author of havoc on earth. The Vulgate renders the Greek Apollyon by the Latin Exterminans (that is, "Destroyer"). The identity of Abaddon with Asmodeus, the demon of impurity, has been asserted but not proved.

Remember there is power in our tongue; there is the power of life and death in what we speak. Do you realize how dangerous that is?

In deliverance, we have run up against this many times, especially when working with cancer victims. What we have discovered is that somehow this spirit is closely connected with people who have spiritual cancer. What do I mean by spiritual cancer? I mean the disease came upon them, not by natural causes such as exposure to asbestos or another carcinogen, but by sin. I am not saying spiritual cancer came upon them necessarily through grumbling; I am saying there is a definite correlation between spiritual disease and issues of the mouth. The other connection is unforgiveness.

Do you see the possible consequences of "venting" to each other? If the enemy can get you to open your mouth and vent or complain, you have just opened the gates to hell. We as a society have fallen into a trap the enemy has laid for us. We have been blinded to the consequences of our actions. So let's close the door to Destroyer by stewarding what we say.

God created us in His image, right? We are spirit beings inside this body that we walk around in. God created the universe with the spoken word. God created us in His image. We create and cause things to happen around us with our mouth.

> A man's stomach[38] [Bosom] shall be satisfied from the fruit[39] [reward]) of his mouth; From the produce of his lips he shall be filled. Death and life are in the power[40] [control] of the tongue, And those who love[41] [ally] it will eat[42] [consume/devour] its fruit[43]. [reward] (Pr 18:20-21 NKJV).

If you want peace in your life, then you must ask yourself, "What am I speaking? What is coming out of my mouth? Is it constructive or destructive?" Death and life are in the power of the tongue.

> And I will give you the keys [symbol of authority] of the kingdom of heaven, and whatever you bind[44] [tie up; declare unlawful] on earth will be bound in heaven, and whatever you loose[45] [dissolve, put off] on earth will be loosed in heaven[46][abode of God, eternity] (Matt. 16:19 NKJV).

I learned a long time ago that in deliverance and healing, you have to make sure to free people from anything that might have been bound to them through gossip, curses or even evil speaking, or past generations, in order to help ensure healing. The point is that we need to pay attention to what comes out of our mouths. We are God's ambassadors here on earth, and we carry supernatural power. Dunamis power. Dynamite spiritual power. We must use this power with great wisdom. We are not to allow anything destructive to come out of our mouth. We create with our mouth. We should be a steward—warden or guardian— over what we say.

There is a little word *venting*. The root of the word *vent* is a four-letter word. Watch out! I want to expose a lie we have all believed. We have bought into the lie that venting is healthy. It is a common thought that releasing frustration through venting is healthy. Let me show you the lie: Scott Norvell defines venting as "the result of a demonic lie that deceives the person into verbally judging the actions of another person."[47] It causes us to verbally spew out of our mouths frustration about another person's actions and how it has affected me, myself, and I. Basically, venting is extremely self-centered and egotistical.

Proverbs says: You will eat the fruit of your mouth. Those things you are speaking have a supernatural consequence. Those words have a cause and effect result.

What you speak will be turned back on yourself. Matt. 7:1-2 tells us, "Judge not, that you be not judged. For with what judgment you judge, you will be judged; and with the measure you use, it will be measured back to you" (KJV). For those of you who lack mercy—you're in trouble.

The question can be asked, "If I am not supposed to vent, then how do I redirect the frustration?" We should consider the other side of the equation. Let's get out of our narrow self and try looking out of others' eyes and their background. Does that person come from a violently abused background? Are they hurt and wounded? Are you adding to it? Matt. 12:7 reminds us, "But if you had known what *this* means, "I desire mercy[48] [compassion, tenderness-] and not sacrifice, you would not have condemned the guiltless" (NKJV).

We should all ask ourselves, "Have I been venting?" If so, let's pray this prayer:

> Lord, You are the God of the Universe and have
> made all things. I honor You today and thank You

for the blood of Jesus. I repent (turn away) from gossip and/or venting and ask forgiveness. I ask You to wash me with the precious blood, that I may be spotless before You.

I loose the word curses I have sent out against any person and cast down every evil work it has created. Including toward myself. I choose to walk in love and mercy toward this person. Lord, I ask You, Lord, to fill me with Your love and mercy for this person.

Thank You, Lord, for forgiving me. I pray Your blessings and protection over all involved.

In Jesus's name. Amen.

THE POWER OF SOUND

For by him [Jesus] all things were created: things in heaven and on earth, visible and invisible, whether thrones or powers or rulers or authorities; all things were created by him and for him. He is before all things, and in him all things hold together (Col 1:16-17, AMP).

The physicist who discovered quarks in an atom was Murray Gell-Mann; he won a Nobel Prize in 1969. He discovered that quarks are permanently confined in the neutron and proton so you cannot pull them out to examine them singly. In quantum mechanics a quark is not exactly a point; it's quite a flexible object. Sometimes it behaves like a point, but it can be "smeared out" a little. Sometimes it behaves like a wave.[49] -Apparently, this made studying quarks difficult as you cannot exactly find them. A scientist can measure the quark's velocity but then is unable to measure its location, and vice versa. And according to the *Urban Dictionary on String Theory*, "String theory states that quarks are made up of tiny vibrating strings.[50]" Hence, even quarks hold sound.

There is power in the spoken word. We are created in His image, a creative being. Therefore, since Jesus formed such unseen things as quarks by speaking them into being, we have a creative force when we speak too. Heb. 11:1 says, "Now faith is the substance of things hoped for, the evidence of things not seen" (KJV). Quarks are part of the unseen that forms creation and holds sound.

> Blessed is the king who comes in the name of the Lord! Peace in heaven and glory in the highest! Some of the Pharisees in the crowd said to Jesus, "Teacher, rebuke your disciples! I tell you," he replied, "if they keep quiet, the stones will cry out" (Luke 19:38-44, NKJV).

Scientists have done studies on the ancient stones at Stonehenge and found the rocks hold sound; in fact, it is like musical notes. "Different sounds can be heard in different places on the same stones,"[51] said the researchers.- What did Jesus say? If His people did not worship, the stones would cry out. Rocks hold musical sound.

There has been research done by a man named Pjotr Garjajev who has proven vibration caused by sound can actually change DNA. What was discovered is that human DNA stores data like a computer's memory system, with our genetic code using grammar rules and syntax just like the human language.[52]- Apparently, through our talking, using sound, vibrations, and frequencies, we can actually change our DNA. In deliverance, we have long since learned that a demon can change a person's DNA, i.e, illness; after the demon is cast out, we are able through prayer and the Holy Spirit to heal the individual. Prayer has a frequency as well. In fact, frequency will rise when a person is in prayer. We are able to help our body heal through pure anointing oils, as they hold a frequency. It is a known fact that when the oils are applied to the body the healing properties of the oil will gravitate to the same frequency in the human body. And when the oil is prayed over, it raises the frequency in the oil.

Dr. Masaru Emoto studied the impact of the power of speech in the process of freezing water. What was discovered was that if the water was spoken to in a negative manner as it froze, it froze in an ugly shape, whereas when water was spoken to in a positive manner, it froze into beautiful artistic shapes. He went on to have a priest pray over the ugly frozen water and to everyone's amazement the shape changed into a beautiful form.[53] There is power in prayer; it changes frequencies. -

Some sounds will pierce the veil between the supernatural and the natural and open gates into the throne room of God—worship and praise. God's Word states, "The Lord dwells in the praises of His people." When we couple the sound of our praises (sound/frequency) with our faith, which pleases God, we will have an extraordinary interaction of the natural with the supernatural. That is where the two worlds collide. It is a key in the Kingdom of God.

To understand the power that interacts with the spoken words that cause vibrations and frequencies to rise and fall in things even as small as a quark, listen to these fateful words that were spoken: "Father, forgive them, for they know not what they do." These words were uttered by Jesus as he hung on the cross. His blood, innocent and without sin, was running down his arms, his side, and feet. The blood resonated with the power of His words! Father, forgive them, ν not what they do. We call on the blood of Jesus to wash us of all sin. I never dreamed that blood contained his words. When we declare the blood of Jesus, we are invoking his words to be put in intercession for us in the throne room of God.

I was in Chiloquin, Oregon, at a conference when I had a vision. I saw the hands of Jesus and they were bleeding. The blood was fresh like it was happening right now, not two thousand years ago. It dawned on me that God is outside of time. Therefore, the past, present, and future are happening simultaneously. The spiritual sacrifice that happened two thousand years ago, for the Lord, is happening right now. He "sees" it fresh, not years ago. The blood containing the frequencies and vibrations of the words "Father, forgive them, they know not what they do" are fresh and right now.

Dear heavenly Father,

Open their eyes, in order to turn them from darkness to light, and from the power of Satan to God, that they may receive forgiveness of sins and an inheritance among those who are sanctified by faith in Me" [Jesus] (Acts 26:18 NKJV).

PART III

SPIRITUAL BODY MAPPING

CHAPTER 7

PREPARATIONS FOR A SESSION

I have found it helpful to prepare not only my spirit through worship and reading the Word before a session; but also to prepare my body.

Fasting

Before a session, I will sometimes "fast." I do not believe in fasting during a session! Let me explain why. Fasting is to prepare me, to get me out of the way of the Lord. I do this ahead of time, as I need my strength both in the spirit and in the natural to minister. When in spiritual warfare it is better to have strength in the spirit and the body.

> But Jonathan heard not when his father charged the people with the oath: wherefore he put forth the end of the rod that was in his hand, and dipped it in a honeycomb, and put his hand to his mouth, and his eyes were enlightened. Then answered one of the people, and said, Thy father straitly charged the people with an oath, saying, Cursed be the man that eateth any food this day. And the people were faint. Then said Jonathan, My father hath troubled

the land: see, I pray you, how mine eyes have been enlightened because I tasted a little of this honey. How much more, if haply the people had eaten freely today of the spoil of their enemies that they found? For had there not been now a much greater slaughter among the Philistines (1 Sam. 14:27-30, KJV).

Diet

Before the session, I will make sure to eat a healthy diet, including proteins, as they will help to maintain stamina.

For every creature of God is good, and nothing to be refused if it be received with thanksgiving: For it is sanctified by the word of God and prayer (1 Tim. 4:4, NKJV).

We are to sanctify our food by the word of God and prayer so that it will nourish our physical bodies. If we are to complete the job the Lord has given to us while we are here on earth, we must take care of the vehicle He has placed our spirit within. The Lord once asked me, "Do you want to drive a Maserati or a VW when you are older?" I knew what He meant. He was giving me a choice. I could take care of my body now and be able to complete my task with grace, with a well-adjusted body, or I could neglect the body and have trouble with it later. It was my choice.

CHAPTER 8

SPIRITUAL BODY MAPPING

What is Spiritual Body Mapping?

Spiritual body mapping is a diagnostic tool for inner healing and deliverance. It is a combination of dream interpretation, sozo, terraforming, old-fashioned deliverance, healing, and territorial warfare. Quite a mouthful, huh? That is the most simplistic way I can describe it. Let us consider the human body to be a map; each part represents a region in the spiritual realm. Each location according to the Word of God represents our path with Him in one form or another.

Spiritual mapping identifies strong points as well as the problem areas in our walk with the Lord. I found a strong connection among our body, spirit, and soul. It would seem that one "tells on" the other. Remember that in the Bible, John stated, "I will say that you be in good health and prosper EVEN as your SOUL [mind, will, and emotions] prosper" (3 John 1:2 NKJV). Wow! John was putting an equal sign between our health and prosperity and how we think. From what I found, what we believe manifests in our body. Scripture illustrates this in 1 Cor 12:12-27 when Paul explains the concept of the body of Christ and how the body should fit together and what will cause a schism within that body. This reference speaks of the church, of how important we are individually as well as corporately.

One person is not over the other person, but we should be jointly fit together, honoring each other's position. I believe our natural body works in a similar fashion. It is like the body of Christ in that each area has a particular meaning and job both in the natural and the supernatural realms. The foot, the hand, the ear, and so on, each have a specific meaning and job..

I began to research what the Bible had to say about our bodies; I used widely accepted scripture and located "first mentions." In other words, I used the theory that a thought mentioned in the Bible the first time sets a precedent as to how it is used throughout the rest of the Bible. Using this as a guideline for "interpreting" concepts, words, colors, items, etc., I began to form a type of dictionary. Since most of the words were found in the Old Testament, their precedence still needed to be brought through the cross of Jesus and visited through the eyes of grace.

A lot of interpreting is needed in mapping a person, as the person will begin to see, feel, smell, taste, and hear spiritually. Please do not try to make interpreting harder than it is. The Lord speaks to man in the most basic form there is—pictures. The most ancient written communication was accomplished through pictures on cave walls. Images will have more meaning than just one word, as a picture is worth a thousand words.

In interpreting, a picture may mean one thing to you but to the individual, it could have an entirely separate meaning. Be sure to check with the person and ask them what the item, picture, or whatever they are experiencing, means to them personally as well as lining it up with the scriptures.

Let me give you an example. A kangaroo usually reminds a person of Australia or down under, whereas to me it speaks of family. When I was a little girl, my mother was getting remarried and took me aside to tell me. I was scared because I did not know if I would get to go with her into this new life. I asked my mother if I could come too. She handed me a small kangaroo that she had bought for me and said, "Yes! We are a package deal." So to me, a kangaroo speaks of family. In a dream a while back, the Lord used a drowning kangaroo to represent to me a family member who needed to be rescued, as this person was spiritually drowning.

During the session, an individual may doubt they hear from the Lord. It is important in the interpretation process of the mapping to work together with the individual. I like to use this time to teach them to recognize the voice of the Lord. Many times they have been hearing Him all along but just did not have understanding. By the time the session is over, the individual will *know* they are hearing from the Lord.

One thing psychology has done is to take away our spiritual sight by calling it our mere imagination and sometimes stating that it is not real. I am not against psychology at all—I love to work with counselors—but let me tell you here and now: To see, hear, and smell in the spirit is very real. We have our five senses in the spirit as well as in the natural world; most of us just have not been taught how to use them or the difference between the two realms. As I have covered earlier, the soul is the mind, will, and emotions, while the spirit is spirit.

Here is a useful yardstick—if you are consciously searching in your mind for answers to the questions asked during the mapping process, then you are in the soul realm. We are not to go seeking the answers to the questions ourselves. We are to wait upon the Lord and allow the answers to be brought to us by the Holy Spirit. If they are from the Holy Spirit, these answers will always line up with the Bible; this is not a matter of the brain working.

The University of Pennsylvania did a study in which scientists hooked electrodes up to an individual's brain. They asked the person to speak and the lobe in the brain that operated speech lit up. The scientists then hooked the electrodes up to another individual and watched as the individual worshipped the Lord in tongues; the electrodes did not light up as before[54]– The person worshipping did so by the spirit!

We are a three-part being, soul, body, and spirit. The three parts that make up the individual should work together. If one part is out of alignment, that is when we have a schism within the individual. That division can cause a lot of restless nights as well as other manifestations.

Each part of the natural body will store spiritual issues, memories, wounds, etc., as well as very positive things about the person. These strengths and issues are often hidden, even from the individual. I remember when I started doing spiritual mapping and how it enhanced our ability to quickly diagnose areas that were prominent in the person as well as uncover areas that needed work. spiritual body mapping will bring affirmation to the individual. Our strengths are encoded in our bodies as well in other aspects of ourselves that may need healing. I have watched people light up like a light bulb after reading their map as they realized their value in the Kingdom of God.

The second thing spiritual body mapping may do is reveal a wound or hurt. When this occurs, we gently locate, open the wound, and identify the legal rights the spirit or wound may have for being present with that person. We then go through a forgiveness process where the individual may need to forgive others as well as him- or herself. The next step is to dislodge and bring healing. Mapping cuts to the chase and goes right to where to start with a person in a session.

There are times when the person we are working with will hit a block. They are unable to see or respond to the questions asked of them. They see and feel nothing. The first thing I will do is ask if they see the color black or dark. Many times the individual does not recognize that to be a color. Almost every time their reply is 'yes'. If the person has a block, another thing I will do is use different anointing oils to unblock them. It is important to know which oil to use in a session, as oils have specific purposes, according to God's design.

After using this technique for a while, I have learned that the mapping will change as counseling and deliverance progresses. It is good to refer periodically back to the map and reassess what is changing in the individual's profile as the person grows in the Lord.

I have already mentioned a couple of things that spiritual body mapping does, but there are other things it does as well.

1. It enhances our ability to diagnose quickly the areas that are strengths in an individual and give direction.
2. It is useful for teaching a person how to use their spiritual five senses and to recognize when the Lord is talking with them. Most people are surprised at how easy this is to do.

Understanding the Map

Let us address the importance of the parts of the body and the location of things in mapping. But, before we begin to discuss each part in the human body, we must first divide the body between the natural and the spiritual. By going to the Bible and using the *Strong's Hebrew Dictionary*, I found that the left side represents the spiritual aspect of a person and the right side represents the natural element.

Left Side

According to *Strong's Hebrew Dictionary*, the word *left* derives from from Strong's number 8040. שְׂמֹאול smo'wl, sem-ole'; or שְׂמֹאול smosl, sem-ole'; The root word is 5566. סֶמֶל çemel, seh'-mel; or סֵמֶל çemel, say'-mel; from an unused root meaning to resemble; a likeness: figure, idol, image.

I immediately thought of Genesis 1:26:

> And God said, Let us make man in our image, after our likeness: and let them have dominion over the fish of the sea, and over the fowl of the air, and over the cattle, and over all the earth, and over every creeping thing that creepeth upon the earth (KJV).

What image would that be? God is spirit, and He created Adam as a companion. To be a friend to God, one must be in the spirit. This is the same today, when we worship Him "in spirit and in truth." John 4:24 says, "God is Spirit and those who worship Him must worship in spirit and in truth" (NKJV).

It is important not to ignore our spirit but to feed and nourish it for it is our spirit man that understands the 'things' of God.

Right Side

According to *Strong's Hebrew Dictionary* the word *right* is Strong's number 3233. יְמָנִי ymaniy, yem-aw-nee'; from 3231; יָמַן yaman, yaw-man'; a primitive root; to be (physically) right (i.e. firm).

I went to the Word to see what the Lord said about this right side.

> And he said unto them, Cast the net on the right side of the ship, and ye shall find. They cast

therefore, and now they were not able to draw it for
the multitude of fishes. (John 21:6 KJV)

What I discovered was that by obeying the Word of the Lord
when He spoke, the disciples experienced blessings in the natural
realm. I definitely believe the spiritual world affects our natural
world. Logically speaking, the spiritual realm was here first.

So now, it is established that the left side deals with the spiritual
focus and the right side deals with the natural focus. I began to
delve into the Bible further, to see what it had to say about the
individual body parts. I wanted to know what each part's function
was. Many times, I had to go to the Greek or Hebrew and even
further into the root meaning of a word to gain understanding.
Noting its representation/function, I developed a template for our
sessions. (See The Body Representation Chart)

I will start the session by addressing the left side of a person, at
the feet, and work up. I will then ask the individual what he or she
might see or sense with his or her spiritual senses. Let me give you an
example. When asked what they sense about the left foot, the person
may state they see a color or an object, or sense a word. Ps 119:105
says, "Thy word is a lamp unto my feet, and a light unto my path"
(KJV), and Luke 1:79 exhorts us "To give light to them that sit in
darkness and in the shadow of death, to guide our feet into the way
of peace" (KJV).

Noting what side of the body I am working with (the left), the
color or object the person is seeing reflects the condition of their
spiritual walk. If it were the right foot we were addressing, the color
or object would reflect the condition of the person's natural walk. I
would then move up to the ankle and repeat the process until I had
covered the whole body. .

THE MAPPING OF A PERSON

Before starting a session, it is crucial to invite the Holy Spirit in, as it is Him who should be directing everything that is said and done. We do this through prayer and worship, as instructed by Ps 100:4: "Enter into his gates with thanksgiving, and into his courts with praise: be thankful unto him, and bless his name" (NKJV). The way into the presence of the Lord is through His gates, which are accessed by offering up thanksgiving and praise and then going deeper into His presence through worship. I have found it helpful to have worship music playing in the background during the session.

As I have stated before, be aware, anytime you are operating in deliverance, inner healing, or for that matter working in the spirit in any capacity, that you will be opening doors into the spirit realm. These doors can be opened into the second heaven but not into to the third heaven, where the throne of God is. The second heaven can be a wild place, as this is where a lot of spiritual warfare takes place. The second heaven is that place between the throne room of the Lord and earth. This is clearly laid out in the Old Testament in Dan 10:12, where the Archangel Gabriel explains to Daniel that the Lord heard him from the time he determined in his heart and prayed. But he then went on to explain the delay in getting the message to Daniel. The evil prince of Persia withstood him twenty-one days. The Archangel Michael came to assist Gabriel in getting through to deliver the message from the Lord. With this said, please close all doors after the session. I cannot begin to tell you how many times my husband and I had spiritual traffic at night in our house because we forgot to close a door.

Now, remembering that the left side of the body represents the spiritual side of the person and the right side represents the natural side of the person, let us begin to examine the parts of our body. I have learned it is best to start with one side and work up through all of the parts on the same side and then start on the other side and work up through all of those parts, and then to examine the midsection of the body.

I ask the Holy Spirit to reveal anything the person needs to see, hear or feel during the session and ask Him to take control. I will start the mapping by asking the person to close their eyes and "look" at their foot in the spirit. I wait and then ask what they saw or heard when I asked them about their foot. Be sure to give them time to hear or see from the Holy Spirit, and do not lead them by making suggestions. Above all, do not rush your session. The person may answer with a color, impression, a feeling or even an object or event. It can be anything. Be observant. Watch the person's facial expressions. If they are frowning while waiting for an answer from the Lord, they may be searching themselves for answers. If so, they are in the soul realm and not in the spirit. Talk to the person and encourage them to relax, and learn to wait on the Holy Spirit. Encourage the person to quiet their mind and spirit (though never making their mind blank). Inform the person that after they are asked a question, they should patiently wait for the answer. They may understand it as a thought popping into their head.

If the person is not hearing, seeing or feeling anything in the spirit, be sure to ask them if they are seeing black or darkness. Sometimes people do not recognize the dark or black to be a color. Be prepared to work outside the box but within the Word of God. If I do not know the meaning or interpretation of their response, I will go to the Bible and do my research. I then write the answer down on the mapping form.

The next step is to uncover the lie, trauma, wound or sin through which the enemy has been able to gain access to the individual's life. This could mean going back in time, as it may be a generational issue. If there is a lie involved, I will ask the person to confess the lie that they came into agreement with in their mind, for instance, "I am fat" or "I am not as smart as others." Once they have confessed the lie, they are to repent for believing the lie and ask the Lord to forgive them, call on the blood of Jesus to wash it all away. The person will usually see a color or something at this point, and you will be able to tell if there is more work needed in this area or if you can to move on. The color white usually will let me know it is time to move on.

If there is trauma involved, I will go back and visit the traumatic situation, seeing it again through the spirit. I will ask the person what they see, feel or are impressed by. It is interesting because in most situations, the event seems low-light, or colors may seem dimmer to the person. What is interesting to me, the person may see a spirit standing near the event. The person will tell the spirit it has to leave and call on the angels. After that is done, the perception of the event will change in the person's spirit. When they picture the previously traumatic event the colors may become brighter and they will not have a pain or tightening in their chest when they think about it.

I will go through all parts of the body until we have covered each item that was brought up in the initial mapping. Again, I have found it extremely helpful to have worship music and intercessors present in a session. All the glory goes to the Lord.

INTERPRETING A BODY MAP

As previously pointed out, the left side represents the spiritual realm for the person and the right side represents the natural realm. Note the body parts and see what the Bible has to say regarding their job and/or meaning, then use discernment and remember that discernment is not criticism. Be sure to ask the person what a picture may mean to them; include them in the interpretation process. The

Lord will use images pertinent them. These images, colors, words, whatever the person perceives will have a direct say regarding the body part and what it represents.

I have included a list of charts to assist you in getting the idea of how to interpret your body map. People have asked me, "Where did you locate the interpretation of the items?" I found them in the Bible either in the English or in the Hebrew/Greek; I researched root words. I also used the Webster's Dictionary and today's vernacular.

* Guidelines for a Session   * General Prayer
* Shapes   * Directions
* Metals   * Weapons/Items
* Stones   * Spirit Location
* Body Parts   * Glossary
* Colors
* Spiritual Body Mapping Template

How to use the charts and templates. First, lead the person through the general deliverance prayer. Then go to the spiritual body map template and write the person's name and date. As you lead them through the session follow the template's order and fill in the blanks. After you have completed the template then go back and begin the interpretation process. I cannot stress enough to include the person in interpreting what was seen, heard and felt. I have left room for interpretation after each section of the body. Feel free to use the charts of various colors, directions, items, etc., as a reference to their meanings.

CHAPTER 9

AFTER A MAPPING SESSION

After the session, it is important to require follow-up appointments for discipleship. Deliverance and inner healing will get rid of the demonic activity in a person's life and address spiritual wounds. But now the habits must be addressed. That means discipline and accountability. To say the least, deliverance is a process, not a single event. Therefore, an individual who has undergone a session will need a spiritual mentor to disciple them. We are called to make disciples, not churchgoers.

Our society today wants a quick fix. James 1 clearly states, "Trials and tribulations work patience." That word *trials* means to "put to proof" and when you continue to read, it has to do with your faith. When we go through these things, it is in order to develop your faith in the Lord. He wants to be there with you. Allow these things that you go through to complete a good work within you. What is the good work within you? James goes on to state, "the testing of your faith produces patience."

Patience is cheerful endurance. The Lord means it to "prove the good with you," not to set you up to fail. As you begin to break down old habits, realize that you are working on developing the character of Christ and good fruit in your life.

Now remember, I am giving you basic guidelines. You have to be led by the Holy Spirit at all times as you walk this out. A person can only produce the fruit of the spirit by the empowering of the Holy Spirit.

After a Session

I like to take B12 tablets to replenish my body's energy. There is another thing to address. That is taking time to rest. I am laughing—I can see your expression as you just read that sentence. I can see you, the reader, saying, "And just how am I supposed to do that?"

The Lord has designed our body to labor on a six-day work week. It is proven that our system works on a higher level for six days than for seven. On the seventh day, our system relaxes. Again, it is your choice; you can take the day off or your body will take time off without your permission. Do you want to drive a Maserati or VW?

It is important after the deliverance to worship the Lord in all that He has accomplished through you. You and He are partners in this ministry. It is a wonder to watch as He moves through you and your team. Be grateful and thankful for a job well done.

Celebrate the Victory

I remember one time I was with the Glory Riders and we had just come out of a huge event that lasted five days. We were weary, battered, and bruised, but we had won with the help of the Lord. As we were caravanning home, I heard the Lord say, "Celebrate the victory." Wow! What amazing words. Immediately, I experienced a download of different victories in the Bible when the men of God would celebrate.

About that time, we were getting ready to pass a favorite restaurant where the team enjoyed stopping to eat. I got on the walkie-talkie and told everyone to pull into the restaurant's parking lot, because the Lord had told us to *celebrate*. I bought everyone their favorite dessert and we celebrated!

Another time, I was wallowing around in the dumps over a situation that happened to me. It was a devastating circumstance. The enemy had pulled out all the stops to try to destroy my family and me. I heard the Lord say, "You should be celebrating the enemy's defeat." Whew, talk about an awaking out of self-pity. I'd been focusing on the wrong thing. I was focusing on my heart's pain when I should have been focusing on the fact that the enemy had been defeated in his plan to destroy my family and me. The adversary's plan had failed.

> Nevertheless do not rejoice in this, that the spirits are subject to you, but rather rejoice because your names are written in heaven. (Luke 10:20, NKJV).

We are not to rejoice that the demons are subject to us; our rejoicing should be in that we are beloved of the Lord and paid for by His blood.

PART IV

COMMONLY ASKED
QUESTIONS

CHAPTER 10

DREAMS, KEYS, AND HUMAN SPIRITS

DREAMS

Dreams are very real, and they are not always just your mind working things out in the night hours. Dreams cross cultural boundaries, yet some cultures give them more credence than others. The Aborigines in Australia hold to the belief that the dreamer has legal ownership of the story.

"In fact, the dream is owned by the dreamer. In the Aboriginal belief, a Dreaming story must be respected as the knowledge held by only the one who dreamed it. No one else can portray in any way that Dreaming story without permission. These stories are the same as if an author had written them down, only they are passed down orally from generation to generation".[55]

The Lord created dreams and uses them to communicate with people. Remember that in Genesis, the Lord came down every evening to talk with Adam. Some people think they don't want to ask the Lord for anything until they need him, as though they are saving up their three wishes for something that is important. But that is not how it is with the Lord and your relationship with Him. He wants to talk to you and you with Him. His desire is to be intimate with you. Here are some of the ways the Lord will communicate with his people.

1. Audible messages, such as in the story of Saul on the road to Damascus
2. Visions, both open and closed visions. An open vision is a vision a person would have with their eyes open, everything around them disappears and they in another setting, whereas a closed vision occurs in the mind's eye.
3. Trances, such as in the story of Peter on the roof
4. Revelation or "light bulb" experiences
5. Angels appearing to men
6. Out-of-body experiences, such as in the story of John on the Island of Patmos
7. Messages from other people, especially prophets
8. Dreams

As we can see, the Lord communicates with us in many different ways, but for the purpose of this book, I will focus on dreams.

> And it shall come to pass in the last days, saith God, I will pour out of my Spirit upon all flesh: and your sons and your daughters shall prophesy, and your young men shall see visions, and your old men shall dream dreams. And on my servants and on my handmaidens I will pour out in those days of my Spirit; and they shall prophesy (Acts 2:17-18, KJV).

The Lord will give dreams for many different reasons. A dream can give direction, answer your questions, and even warn you of danger.

When they had gone, an angel of the Lord appeared to Joseph in a dream. "Get up," he said, "take the child and his mother and escape to Egypt. Stay there until I tell you, for Herod is going to search for the child to kill him" (Matt 2:13, NIV).

Dreams come from three different sources. The first source is the Lord, coming to talk to you at night. Personally, I believe that He will do this because in dreams he can speak directly to your spirit. That is not to say he cannot do that during the day, but at night we are quiet and still.

The second source is the enemy.

"Behold, I am against them that prophesy false dreams, saith the LORD, and do tell them, and cause my people to err by their lies, and by their lightness; yet I sent them not, nor commanded them: therefore they shall not profit this people at all," saith the LORD (Jer. 23:32, NIV).

And the third source is your soul. Some psychologists believe this is our mind working out daily activities and problems.

How do you recognize what the source of a dream is? There are several things you can do to discern the origin. First of all, try the spirit; does it line up with the Word of God? Whom does the dream lift up? What is the result or fruit of the dream? Is it constructive or destructive? If the dream makes you feel important or if the dream seems to be lining up the Bible but is slightly askew, it is from the enemy. If the dream lines up perfectly with the Word of God, then it is from the Lord. Some would assume if it is scary then it is from Satan, but that is not necessarily true. The Lord may be warning you of a situation you are involved in or that is coming toward you, or he may be revealing that you are wrestling an unclean or evil spirit.

When you begin to interpret your dreams, the first thing you will want to do is to keep a notepad and pencil beside the bed so you can write your dreams down. I like to date my dreams and make notes as to what is going on in my life at the time. I have found that to helpful in interpreting. Also, write down the feelings you had within the dream. The Lord will use pictures that have a personal meaning to you. So when you interpret a picture, ask yourself, "What does this mean to me?"

For example, I trained horses for many years; therefore, the Lord may use a breed of horse to emphasize a point; a thoroughbred horse would speak to me of speed and endurance, whereas, a quarter horse would represent quick speed and strength but not necessarily endurance. The Lord is intimate and knows your heart; each dream is personal to you. I will also go to the Bible to see what a picture might mean and to see how it is used in the scriptures. Always invite the Holy Spirit into the interpretation process.

In the interpretation process, usually the first scene is what the Lord wants to talk to you about, and then the rest of the dream pertains to that subject matter.[56-] If the setting is the same as in real life, then you would have a tendency to interpret the dream literally; if the setting is not like real life, the dream can probably be interpreted as a parable.[57] Pay close attention to details such as directions, who is driving the car, colors, etc. We have a detail-oriented God; one just has to look at creation itself to discern that.

You can change the outcome of the dream. Just because a dream occurs in one way does not mean you have to accept that.[58] Through dreams, the Lord may reveal a situation ahead of time so that you can pray into the future and change the outcome. The Lord may be exposing the enemy's hand or exposing something that is in your heart, which is in your power to change either through actions or prayer, or both.

Just a thought here—do not be too quick to interpret a dream. Sometimes a dream comes with a pause or comma. In other words, it may be a two- or three-part dream. You may have a connecting dream in the next night or two. Wait on the Lord in interpreting the dream and ask Him for the interpretation. Be sure to interpret the dream through the eyes of grace. We are under grace, not the law.

Keys

There are keys referred to in the Bible, each of which has authority. It is essential for us to be aware of these keys and of who has the authority to use which keys. There are four keys the Lord gave back to man upon His ascension.

> And I will give you the keys [symbol of authority] of the kingdom of heaven, and whatever you <u>bind</u>[59] [tie up, declare unlawful]- on earth will be bound in heaven, and whatever you <u>loose</u>[60] [untie, declare lawful]- on earth will be loosed in heaven[61]. [abode of God, eternity]- (Matt. 16:19, NKJV).

The keys the Lord gave to man:

1. Binding and Loosing (Matt 16:19)
    I learned a long time ago, in deliverance and healing, that you have to make sure to free people from anything that might have them bound, through words or actions, and then go into the past generations to do the same, loosing strongholds from bloodlines. You will also want to loose the generational blessings, allowing them to flow. Sin in

the past generations can stop or slow down the abundant blessings. The enemy will try to choke off those blessings either legitimately or illegitimately, and unless someone calls him on it, he will do it!

The flip side of loosing is binding. You have the authority to bind the enemy. But be aware, he has the power to restrict you if you become an aggressor in an attack. The enemy has the right, just as you do, to self-defense. The spiritual laws are for all involved, not just for mankind. You can bind such things as spirits, situations, and people. You can also bind locations. We are God's ambassadors here on earth and with that we carry supernatural power. Dunamis power. Dynamite spiritual power. We must use this authority with great wisdom.

2. The key of knowledge (Luke 11:52)

    The Lord talked about the key of knowledge to the lawyers and how they withheld knowledge from others. Not only that, but they did not use it either. Luke 11:52 says, "Woe unto you, lawyers! for ye have taken away the key of knowledge: ye entered not in yourselves, and them that were entering in ye hindered" (KJV).

    Upon further study, you will find the key of knowledge to be the secret things that belong to the Lord. Deut. 29:29 says, "The secret things belong unto the LORD our God: but those things which are revealed belong unto us and to our children for ever, that we may do all the words of this law" (NKJV). The Lord wants his children to have revelations so that we are able to "do all the words of this law." When we take this verse through the cross into the

New Testament we find the number one law that covers all others is to love.

> And thou shalt love the Lord thy God with all thy heart, and with all thy soul, and with all thy mind, and with all thy strength: this is the first commandment. And the second is like, namely this, Thou shalt love thy neighbour as thyself. There is none other commandment greater than these. And to love him with all the heart, and with all the understanding, and with all the soul, and with all the strength, and to love his neighbor as himself, is more than all whole burnt offerings and sacrifices (Mark 12:30 KJV).

Therefore, we see the key of knowledge to be revelation from the Holy Spirit, but note the close connection with the law of love.

In Luke 11:52, there is definitely a warning regarding this key. Jesus admonished the lawyers because they hindered others from attaining the key of knowledge, manifesting signs of pride; Leviathan is over the sons of pride and tries to keep others from the river of revelation.

3. Key of our Testimony

The key of our testimony is our victory key. Rev 12:11 says, "And they overcame him by the blood of the Lamb, and by the word of their testimony; and they loved not their lives unto the death" (KJV).

The enemy hates our testimony. Our testimony gives us spiritual legal rights. If you break down the word *testimony*, this is what it is: It is a compound of the word *mound*, as in to pile up stones as a memorial or remembrance, and *testify*, which means "to give evidence," as in a courtroom.

We can overcome the enemy legally with the blood of the lamb. Jesus's shedding His blood on the cross, and us accepting His sacrifice and accepting Him as our savior, ceremonially cleanses us from all unrighteousness and puts us in right standing before the Father in heaven. Therefore, we stand clean in the throne room of heaven. We are overcomers by the blood of the lamb and the word of our testimony.

The keys the Lord holds are as follows:

1. The key of David (Rev 3:7 and Is 22:22)

   The key of the house of David

I will lay on his shoulder; So he shall open, and no one shall shut; And he shall shut, and no one shall open (Is. 22:22, NKJV).

Once, I had been fasting for days, and I asked the Lord, "What is this about the key of David? I understand it opens doors that man cannot open and closes them as well. I also understand that it has to do with government; but what does that look like?"

He took me to Is 11:2-5:

The Spirit of the LORD shall rest upon Him,
The Spirit of wisdom and understanding,
The Spirit of counsel and might,
The Spirit of knowledge and of the fear of the LORD.
His delight is in the fear of the LORD,
And He shall not judge by the sight of His eyes,
Nor decide by the hearing of His ears;
But with righteousness He shall judge the poor,

And decide with equity for the meek of the earth;
He shall strike the earth with the rod of His mouth,
And with the breath of His lips He shall slay the wicked.
Righteousness shall be the belt of His loins (NKJV).

It all made sense to me—everything in Is 11:2-5 would be a key;
this key belongs to Jesus.

2. Keys to hell and death (Rev.1:18)
    The Lord also holds the keys to hell and death. Rev.
1:18 says, "I am he that liveth, and was dead; and, behold, I
am alive for evermore, Amen; and have the keys of hell and
of death" (KJV). That is why we do not have to fear death
if we have accepted Him as our Savior. Praise the Lord! In
Matt 16:18, we read that the Lord told Peter in regards to
building His church that the gates of hell would not be able
to defeat it. In other words, the government or principalities
of hell and Hades would not be able to conquer what the
Lord has established.

    It is important to know the keys and their authority and
who holds which keys. We hold the keys of binding and
loosing, the key of knowledge, and the key of our testimony.
The Lord holds the keys of David, hell, and Hades.

HUMAN SPIRITS

People frequently ask me, "Do we have authority over human
spirits?" I am first going to qualify my answer by saying, for the sake
of this section, that the human spirit that I will be addressing is "out
of body." We need to understand astral projection from a Christian
point of view.

First of all, what is astral projection? It is the ability of one's spirit to exit one's physical body and travel. For some people who have exited their body, upon looking back at the body, they report seeing a silver light between their spirit and their physical body. There are some issues involved in doing this:

1. Depending on mind frame, one can draw dark spirits on the other side to them during the projection process and after;
2. There have been reports of spirits getting lost;
3. Others have found their bodies buried while they were out traveling.

For a Christian to astral project, to get out of their body on their own volition, is not good. But there are a couple of places in the Bible where this experience is instigated by God. One such instance is in 2 Corinthians, where Paul states that he knew someone but wasn't sure if he was in the body or out of the body. The second occurrence is in the Rev 1, where John states that he is not certain whether he was in the body or out of the body. Therefore, the Lord can cause an occurrence for the purpose of allowing one to see the things of God.

If you leave your body, always ask yourself, What was the motive of the heart? Was this experience for the things of God or not? What was fruit of it? Did it bring glory to God or was it born out of curiosity?

Every time I have dealt with someone in a deliverance situation that has "projected," I have found an opening at the back of their neck. I discovered this opening quite by accident. I was praying for a girl, and it came out in the session that she had astral projected. I was standing behind her and put my hand on the back of her neck, and my hand in the spirit went inside of her neck. I jumped back; I was so startled. I realized that by her allowing this hole, she had left an opening for future projections. During her session, I closed that opening.

Now for the question, Do we have authority over these human spirits? Let me show you a couple of different cases with different variables.

In Rebecca Brown MD's book *He Came to Set the Captive Free*, she experienced Satanists who were astral projecting to hurt her. The Lord woke her before they got to her house and told her to get out immediately. He did not tell her to stand her ground and rebuke them.

What I observed about her particular situation was:

1. She was a new Christian at the time and without any experience in spiritual warfare
2. She was alone with no backup and outnumbered

I believe that in her case, the wisest course was to get out of Dodge!

Years ago, there was an ex-witch interviewed on a televangelist's program. This ex-witch and the minister were talking about human sacrifices. She was explaining how the Satanists went about choosing their sacrifice. The Satanist would astral project and walk onto a school playground. They would begin to look for their victim. The minister said, "I am sure you could not touch a Christian's child, right?"

The woman replied, "Oh yes, we could!" Then she went on to explain that there were children they were unable to get near and how to protect your child against this type of assault. She said the parents who prayed for their children every day, told the enemy to keep his hands off of them, and called the angels in to protect their child rendered their children safe. It was like there was a force field around them.

The next case I want to share with you is one I experienced years ago as a young minister. I received a phone call from the woman for whom I was an armor bearer. She explained that we had a very unusual case, and she needed my help. This girl's family was from overseas, and her mother was a high priestess of a coven. The family was infamous, and there had even been a TV series on them. The mother had contacted my friend out of desperation, as her daughter was slowly going insane. Remember that what sin walks in the parent runs in the child? Well, here was a prime example.

The mother was flying in with the daughter that night and my friend wanted to know if I would come with her to the airport to meet these two women. I agreed to go.

Now you need to picture this. Here is my friend who is sixty-something and five foot two, and then there is me, twenty-two years old and five foot nine. She and I are standing side by side in the airport waiting for the other two women to arrive. No one had to tell me who the ladies were in the crowd of people, because as the two women drew closer to us, the hair on the back of my neck and arms stood straight up. I couldn't help myself, I sidestepped behind my friend and tried to make myself the size of a mouse. I thought, *What have I gotten myself into?* I watched in horrible fascination as the mother and daughter approached. The daughter's tongue kept flickering out of her mouth like a snake's tongue as we introduced ourselves. That was the introduction to "Amy" (I changed her name for her protection).

Amy stayed with my friend and her mother flew home. In no time at all, my friend would hear footsteps in the hallway of her home and knew it was Amy's mom checking up on her. My friend would tell her to go back home, and the human spirit would leave.

Well one night, the mother, in spirit form, decided to visit me. I remember opening my eyes to see what seemed to be an illuminated ball hovering about three feet off the ground from my bed. I rebuked her and told her to leave—she left.

Human spirits have appeared in their human form as well, as in the case of my grandfather, who appeared at the foot of my bed one night.

It took two years working of with Amy on a daily basis and many times of strong believers coming together in prayer and fasting to set her free. But in the end, she now lives a normal life with the Lord.

So do I feel we have authority over human spirits? Yes and no; it all depends on the variables.

CHAPTER 11

TAKING AUTHORITY OVER CHILDREN, ANIMALS, AND AREAS

Praying over a Child

Many people have asked me about how to pray over a child who is tormented by evil visitations. First of all, get permission from the child's spiritual covering—their parents. I do not pray over a child whose parents are not in agreement.

It is important not to scare the child. If he or she is young, I pray very gently, not making a big deal out of anything. I pray as if I am praying for anything else, but will kindly mention in the middle of prayer, as if by the way, that all foul, unclean, evil or demonic spirits are bound and commanded to leave in Jesus's name, and then will go on and pray for something else. If I am unable to do that, I will tell the parent to pray over them while the child is sleeping. Again, it is all about not scaring the child.

If the child is afraid of his or her room, while the child is away the parent and I will go into the room and spiritually clean it out. Please see the chapter on praying over a house.

A few years back, Mom and I had the occasion to minister to a four-year-old girl who was being tattooed and marked for a satanic ritual and sacrifice. The child's father was a Satanist, and her mother was paralyzed by fear and was, therefore, incapable of saving her daughter from the situation.

The grandmother, a believing Christian, kidnapped the child from their home while the father was away and fled with her to California. She contacted a church, but they did not have any experience in dealing with someone in her situation. The pastor referred her to a church in another city where my mother was attending and ministering in the women's department. The associate pastor knew my mother and our involvement in the deliverance ministry. He immediately telephoned Mom and arranged an appointment for the woman and child.

When they arrived, we sat down and explained the process that was necessary to set this little girl free from all the curses and demonic activity surrounding her since birth. We were able to pray for the little girl, as the child's mother and grandmother were in agreement with us and supported the child's deliverance of the tormenting spirits. We explained that due to the age of the child, we would be extremely careful so she would not be frightened. We spent, off and on, about four hours with the girl.

The grandmother telephoned the next day and was totally amazed and thankful. She informed us that the child had slept through the night without waking once or being restless. That was something she had never experienced in her short little life.

PRAYING OVER ANIMALS

I cannot tell you how many times I have been asked, "Do animals have a spirit?"

> For that which befalleth the sons of men befalleth beasts; even one thing befalleth them: as the one

dieth, so dieth the other; yea, they have all one breath; so that a man hath no preeminence above a beast: for all is vanity. All go unto one place; all are of the dust, and all turn to dust again. Who knoweth the spirit of man that goeth upward, and the spirit of the beast that goeth downward to the earth? (Eccl 3:19-22 KJV)

God, who made the world and everything in it, since He is Lord of heaven and earth, does not dwell in temples made with hands. Nor is He worshiped with men's hands, as though He needed anything, since He gives to all life, breath, and all things (Acts 17:24-25 NKJV).

I looked up the word *all* in the *Mounce Greek Concordance* and it said, "πᾶς *pas* meaning - all, entirety," which means everything that breathes. So whether an animal has a spirit or not is not a "hill I want to die on." In other words, it is not worth causing a division between me and a brother or sister in the Lord.

Now if you ask my personal opinion, then my answer is that I believe they possess a soul (mind, will, and emotions). Demons will choose to torment, oppress or occupy an animal if they cannot have a human. Their first choice is always to have a human, as they call a human their 'house'. In Mark 5:1-14, the demons went into the pigs only after they were cast out of the human.

I remember one time I received a phone call from a woman who ranched in central California. I had trained many of her horses, and I knew her to have outstanding bloodlines. She said, "Carolyn, I have a horse for you. But I want you to know I have sent her to three other trainers and they say she is untrainable." Just what a trainer wants to hear, that three other men have tried to ride this mare and she has bucked them all off. She went on to tell me the horse's pedigree and that she felt she was worth one more chance. I agreed to take the mare on and see what I could do.

The mare arrived, and she was a beauty, no doubt about it. She was coal black, not a white spot on her, and her confirmation was exquisite. But when I looked into her eye, I thought, *Oh boy, here we go.*

The next day, I took her into my round pen, which was forty feet in diameter, had eight-foot solid walls and four to six inches of sand. I walked the mare through the tall gate and closed it behind us, my heart holding tremendous trepidation. I took her to the center of the pen and stood directly in front of her; if you know anything about horses, you know this is not advisable. I put one hand on one side of her cheek and the other hand on the other side of her cheek. I looked her right in the eye and commanded the evil spirit that had hold of her to come out in the name of Jesus Christ. Thirty days later, my pastor's wife was pleasure riding her—she was a sweet mare.

Another encounter I had with demons and an animal was not too long ago. My daughter and I decided that Dad needed a dog. We took Robert to the pound to find the perfect dog. We wandered through the rows of dogs barking and jumping on the wire, trying to get our attention. At first, we did not see any that jumped out at us as though saying, "I'm your dog!" But for some reason, I just could not leave. I strolled through the dog runs for the third time and, at the far end, I saw him. This dog was sitting pressed up against the side of the pen, trying to become invisible; he was not making a sound. The look in his eyes was one of sorrow and grief. I called my husband over, pointed out the dog, and asked him what he thought. Was this his dog? Robert examined him and said, "I like him," and Sam came home with us.

The dog seemed to settle in, but the look in his eyes did not change. He was obviously grieving. One day, I'd had enough of this precious dog being tormented. I laid my hand upon his head and commanded the spirit of sorrow and grief off of him. A few hours later, he was a different dog. Sam is with us to this day— part of our pack.

So yes, demons can torment an animal; and yes, the animals can be delivered. You have authority in the name of Jesus to cast spirits out of your pets.

Praying over a House

Many times, we are asked to go to someone's home and pray over it. This is more common than you might think. Spirits can gain access into our homes through various avenues, such as people, items, generational hand-me-downs, and even the television. My brother took a picture in his living room while the television was on and we could clearly see the full head of a wolf coming out of the screen. The program he had on was a well-known children's program.

A spirit can gain access by attaching itself to an inanimate object. A familiar spirit will gain access to individuals by objects being passed down through the generations, and so can other types of spirits. I urge you to be careful when buying used items and bringing them home without praying over them first. Some items simply cannot be spiritually cleaned and, therefore, they must be disposed of.

When going to pray over a house, set your team up as I have outlined in the territorial warfare chapter of this section. If the Lord leads you to fast, then fast. When we arrive at a person's house we are to pray over, we make sure to have the invitation of the person who is the spiritual covering. If that person is not in agreement, you may or may not get the whole thing done.

The team and I will open a door or window at one end of the house and then proceed to start praying at the other end. We will command all foul, unclean, evil or demonic spirits out in Jesus's name. We keep our eyes open for anything that leaps up at us, such as books and pictures that may allow legal access into the home. Some of the places we thoroughly check out are those that seem exceptionally cluttered, or dark, damp places. If the Lord does point out something in the room, we will then bring the item to the owner's attention and ask them about it. It is up to the owner to discard it. We will move around the room and anoint all openings with the oil, including windows, doors, vents, pipes, and even toilets. Make sure to spiritually clean out closets. Work through the house until you get to the open door or window. Then seal the house with the oil and the blood of Jesus and thank the Lord for His protection.

After we have prayed over the house and sealed it, we will then proceed to the outside grounds. We will start in the middle of the property and pour anointing oil and begin the process I described in the territorial warfare chapter of this section. Things I will look for when praying for a person's property are buried items, spiritual portals, curses, and any defilement that is on the land.

Buried objects can be a very big issue as I learned in a case years ago. At the time, we were attending a large church that had 14,000 members. This particular Sunday, while the service was being televised live, a young girl dressed in black walked through the main doors and up the center aisle to the pastor as he was delivering his message. She told him she wanted to be saved. He smiled and motioned for one of the female prayer partners to go with her and pray with her. About that time, she dropped to her knees and grabbed the amazed pastor by the calves, hanging on for dear life, and announced she was the woman in Revelation. The prayer team took her to one of the prayer rooms to minister to her. My mother was sitting in the service and saw the whole thing happen. She watched as the people took the girl to the back, knowing there was demonic activity afoot. The girl ended up in the hospital.

A few months went by before my mentor received a phone call from this same girl's mother; she was desperate and asked for help. We went to the mother's house to see what the Lord wanted to do. That day it was 110 degrees and there was no breeze; I remember that well. As we were talking in the living room with her mother, the house shook like crazy rattling the windows. My mentor spoke to the room and said, "Knock it off!" Immediately the shaking stopped. We continued to interview the mother and found out she had been angry with her husband and had visited a witch in Mexico. The witch had given her an item to bury in the back yard. The husband died four months later, and her daughter started seeing spirits around the house. Remember what I said, "What walks in the parents will run in the children." So now the daughter was dealing with insanity. We told the mother that she had to repent for what she had done, dig up the item, and destroy it. The mother obediently dug up the cursed statue and disposed of it. After working with the daughter for some time, we finally delivered her; she was healed and finished her degree at Berkley University in California.

When praying over a person's land, I will ask the owner questions about the past regarding the property to gain more insight on issues that may need to be addressed. I will be sure to release any spirits bound to the land. I had a personal experience with an Indian spirit bound to our land. As I was cleaning the property of unwanted weeds I would find bricks buried in the ground, it did not make sense there had not been anything to my knowledge that would explain the bricks. We began to experience spiritual activity. My husband was working as an air traffic controller and used to work shifts at night. The nights he would work, I would hear footsteps walking down the hallway. However, this would not happen when he was home.

It was not long before I called my mom and asked her to help me spiritually clean the house and land. A day or two later, Mom and her friend came up to pray over everything. I explained to the two women that there was an Indian man who walked the hallway at night. We began the process of cleansing the house and land. As we did so, Mom saw a woman in a long lavender dress; the dress appeared to be from around 1900. The three of us released both spirits from the land and things quieted down.

A few months went by, and we had a local repairman come out to fix our television set. He knew the history of our property and the surrounding area. Apparently, the Indians had traveled through our area, migrating up and down the mountain with the seasons. He went on to inform us that around the turn of the century, a woman lived here who made bricks. I about fell off the couch that explained the buried bricks. I immediately knew that spirit was that woman's.

PRAYING OVER TERRITORIES

Before I start on the subject of praying over a territory, I want first to warn you. Some things an individual should not pursue alone, and one of them is this. Territorial warfare is a whole different ballgame from just casting a demon out. In this type of deliverance, you will come against higher-ranked spirits who will not hesitate to stand "toe to toe" with you and call in reinforcements. Some people believe we should not be doing this type of warfare at all.

I remember a time when my head intercessor wanted to do territorial warfare around us. I advised her to please wait for our church to become better trained in spiritual warfare before attempting such an endeavor. I knew our church was not ready for the ramifications of such actions. One night, I received a phone call, and the voice on the other end said one of the people from our church was hurt and in the emergency room. I jumped in the car and headed to the hospital. While in the hospital, I received another phone call; a second accident had occurred and another injured person from the church was now in the same emergency room. I visited with the two individuals and prayed with them. Our associate pastor had heard about the incidents as well and was visiting. While we were there, I received a third phone call; and another accident had happened and a third injured member of our church had been admitted to the hospital across town. Our associate pastor and I jumped in our vehicles and headed out to pray over that person. I remember asking the Lord on the way, "What is going on?" He immediately pointed out to me that someone in our church was doing territorial warfare.

If you feel the Lord is calling you into territorial warfare, then I would like to point out a few things you may want to know.

First, what is the purpose of doing the territorial warfare? If you are looking to set areas free from the bondage of sin, then you are on the right track. The spirits that are in control of a zone will influence the families and homes under their dominion. But please make sure the Lord is telling you to do this.

Second, I would advise you to do a "spiritual map" of the area by looking at the history of the area and noting what has happened in that area, whether it is a blessing or a curse. As you study the history, you will begin to see a pattern of sin or of history repeating itself. This history will give you a clue as to what spirit is controlling that area. You will know the Kingdom of God is manifesting in an area when the evil spirits lose control by the decline of that particular sin.

Set up your team. You should have a team of two to three members who have a clear understanding of warfare. It is also important that any spiritual doors in their lives are closed, so that there is not a legal door for the enemy to come in. Be sure to appoint a leader of the group; the enemy is notorious for causing disunity in the team. And above all, make sure you have intercessors praying for you and the job at hand.

I believe in fasting a few days ahead of time, to ensure my flesh is under control and that I am out of the way of the Lord's will. I will never fast during the battle. The day you are going to pray over the territory, be sure to eat protein, including B12. The additional vitamin will help to maintain your stamina and clear mind.

When it comes time to pray for the land, the team and I will walk to the center of it and pour anointing oil on the ground. I will ask forgiveness for all sins committed on that land and call on the blood of Jesus to cleanse it. I will then declare that all foul, unclean, demonic, evil or human spirits are no longer welcome and, therefore, must leave. I will also call all spirits that are tied to the ground to be untied and released. All unclean soul ties and curses are broken and disavowed.

Something you may want to consider is to make sure a spiritual gate is open for them to pass through. I have had spirits tell me they are unable to leave because they cannot pass through another spirit's territory. I will then open a door through the other spirit's domain and close it after the spirit exits.

I will begin to walk or drive the boundaries of the territory, anointing and inviting the Lord into the area, I will ask Him to bless the land and declare the land for the Kingdom of God. Be sure to anoint corner posts and gates. Do not hesitate to ask for angelic help.

The next thing I will do is clear the heavenlies above and the earth underneath, then close with thanking the Lord for His protection and involvement in setting the land free.

A few years ago, there was a group that did this in our area. At the time, there was a serial killer who was hiding in our mountains and the police could not find him. He had been hiding for four months. After our prayer team had cleansed the territory, that killer was found within a few hours!

Spiritual Boundaries

A few years ago, I received a phone call from a minister in Washington. He was concerned because his son was moving into a house where the previous occupants were into witchcraft; he asked if we could fly up and cleanse the house and land. I agreed to bring my team and see what we could do.

I immediately began to pray, asking the Lord for his wisdom; the Lord gave me a vision of a pitchfork, tongs up. I did not understand it until we got to Washington.

When we arrived on the property, the hair stood up on my arms and my throat constricted; it felt like something was watching me. My team and I were definitely on high alert.

The team and I entered the house through the front door, leaving it open, and began to move toward the back of the house. When we entered the bedrooms, we found trash, torn-up bedding, semen on the walls, etc. We began to pray, anointing, rebuking, and casting out spirits. When we reached the hallway, I looked up to see the opening to the attic above our heads. I informed the men who were assisting us (both Marines) that we needed to go into the attic. I laugh when I recall their response; they turned sheet white and stared back at me. I smiled at them and said I would go. Immediately, both would have none of that; they offered to go first. They both checked out the attic and then allowed me to go up. I found pictures that needed to be destroyed, and we moved on to the next room.

When we reached the living room, I began to walk around the edge of the room praying, and as I reached the far side, my hand went through a spiritual wall, the air becoming frigid. Where I was standing was warm, but where I was holding my hand was freezing. I followed the spiritual boundary around to the outside of the house; it was a definite line of demarcation. I called the pastor over, who was praying off by himself, and told him to hold out his hand. He jumped back startled; "What is that?" he exclaimed. I explained it was a spiritual boundary. The pastor later told me that he had not been sure he believed in that sort of thing—until this happened.

We took authority over the boundary and broke its hold on the land. As we walked around the outside of the barn, I found the pitchfork, lying tongs up buried in the dirt, just as the Lord had shown me in the vision.

The enemy will try to set spiritual boundaries for control over an area. When you run into one of these, look for items, sin, etc., that give legal rights to the enemy to possess the land.

I attended a ministry conference in a well-known town in Arizona. The Lord had warned the leadership, through prayer, what we would be facing before we went. In the spirit, there was a rider dressed in black mounted on a black horse, who rode into town daily. This rider on the black horse was an evil spirit who walked the town.

While we were there, my prayer partners and I decided to walk down the street and pray over the town. We stopped at the major intersection and poured anointing oil. As we prayed, we heard the Lord say, "Anoint the water." We had no idea where to locate the city well. We continued down the street, praying as the Lord led us.

We came to a cross street, and I heard the Lord say, "They are opening a gate to hell." I looked down the street and saw someone was tearing an opening in the side of an old building. My friends and I prayed over the area and called down a firewall to seal the spiritual opening. "'For I,' saith the LORD, 'will be unto her a wall of fire round about, and will be the glory in the midst of her'" (Zechariah 2:5 KJV).

As we passed the town bar, which is well known for having approximately twenty-seven spirits, I asked the Lord if He wanted me to go in. He said, "No, they (the townsmen) want them (the spirits)." So we continued past the bar.

We continued to pray and walk the street; we must have looked like the Desperados walking in a line down the middle of that town. When I looked up, much to my surprise, I saw a tall cowboy, dressed in black, walking down the street directly at me. I immediately knew this was the spirit the Lord had previously warned us about. I stood my ground and waited. He walked right at me, expecting me to move out of his way. I stood. At the last minute, he touched his hat and stepped around us. I let out a sigh of relief, and then the girls and I continued on our way.

At one point, the lady who lived there and was praying with us got agitated and said, "You are headed right for the witch's house!" I had already felt the Holy Spirit lead us to cross to the opposite side of the street from where the witch lived. I asked the Lord about the spiritual boundary and the witch; what did He want us to do? He did not want me to touch it; both the witch and boundary apparently had a legal right to be there. I turned to the agitated lady and told her she needed to return to the conference. I knew we could not have her with us, as the fear would be an opening for the enemy. She and her friend returned to the conference room. My prayer partners and I continued toward the town well and anointed the water.

We were not able to take down the spiritual boundary of the witch or cast out the spirits in the bar, as the people were making money off the notoriety and wanted to keep them.

APPENDIX

Thank you, Lord, for dying for my sins, for glorious resurrection, and for making me a new creature in Christ, by faith in Your precious blood.

Dear Lord, I have a confession to make. I have sought supernatural experiences apart from you. I have disobeyed Your word. I want You to help me renounce all these things, and cleanse me in body, soul, and spirit, in Jesus's name.

I renounce witchcraft and magic, both black and white. I renounce Ouija boards and all other occult games. I renounce all séances, clairvoyance, and mediums, e.s.p., second sight, and mind reading. I renounce all fortune telling, palm reading, tea leaf reading, crystal balls, tarot, and other card laying. I renounce all astrology, new age pursuits, and interest in horoscopes. I renounce the heresy of reincarnation, yoga, and all healing groups involved in metaphysics. I renounce all hypnosis under any excuse or authority.

I break any curse placed on me or my family line from any source, occult or otherwise, in Jesus's name. I break all unclean or demonic soul ties between myself and any other person. I renounce and reject any and all sexual perversion, in Jesus name.

I renounce all curiosity about either future or past, and all that is outside Thy will. I renounce all waterwitching, or dowsing, levitation, body lifting, table tipping, psychometry, and automatic writing. I renounce astral projection, and other demonic skills. I renounce all literature I have ever read in any of these fields and vow that I will destroy such books in my own possession.

I now break, in the name of Jesus Christ, all psychic heredity, and any demonic hold upon my family line, as a result of the disobedience of any of my ancestors. I break any bonds of physical or mental illness, in Jesus's name. I also break all demonic subjection to my mother, father, grandparents or any other human being, in the name of Jesus Christ. I break any unclean or demonic soul ties created or inherited between me and any other person or animal.

I renounce everything psychic and occult. I renounce every philosophy that denies the divinity of Christ. I renounce every cult that denies the blood of Christ.

I call upon the Lord to set me free.

Lord, I have another confession to make. I have not loved, but have resented, certain people. I call upon the Lord to help me forgive them. I do now forgive ... ... (forgive living or dead). I do now forgive myself.

I renounce every evil spirit that torments me and I call upon the Lord to set me free.

(leader says this)

In the name and authority of the Lord Jesus Christ, I come against you, Satan, and all foul, unclean, evil or demonic spirits tormenting this person. I bind you and command you to name yourselves and come out, in Jesus's name, ruler spirits first.

Spiritual Body Map Template

Date: _____;

SPIRITUAL BODY MAPPING of_____

LEFT SIDE OF THE BODY:

Left foot
color: _____ shape: _____ word: _____
Path/walk

Left ankle
color: _____ shape: _____ word: _____
Faith

Left calf
color: _____ shape: _____ word: _____
Running after

Left knee
color: _____ shape: _____ word: _____
Submission

Left thigh
color: _____ shape: _____ word: _____
Covenant/strength of stance

Left hand
color: _____ shape: _____ word: _____
Power/dominion/works

Left arm
color: _____ shape: _____ word: _____
Strength

Left shoulder
color: _____ shape: _____ word: _____
Weight carried/government/authority

Left hip
color: _____ shape: _____ word: _____
Balance

Left ear
color: _____ shape: _____ word: _____
What you hear/listening to

LEFT SUMMARY: _____

_____

_____

_____

_____

_____

_____

_____

_____

_____

RIGHT SIDE OF THE BODY:

Right foot
color: _____ shape: _____ word: _____
Path/walk

Right ankle
color: _____ shape: _____ word: _____
Faith

Right calf
color: _____ shape: _____ word: _____
Running after

Right knee
color: _____ shape: _____ word: _____
Submission

Right thigh
color: _____ shape: _____ word: _____
Covenant/strength of stance

Right hand
color: _____ shape: _____ word: _____
Power/dominion/works

Right arm
color: _____ shape: _____ word: _____
Strength

Right shoulder
color: _____ shape: _____ word: _____
Weight carried/government/authority

Right hip
color: _____ shape: _____ word: _____
Balance

Right ear
color: _____ shape: _____ word: _____
What you hear/listening to

RIGHT SUMMARY: _____
_____
_____
_____
_____
_____
_____
_____
_____

Stomach
color: _____ shape: _____ word: _____
Core of being/reproduction

Chest
color: _____ shape: _____ word: _____
Heart/what is being nurtured or hidden in the heart

Back
color: _____ shape: _____ word: _____
Past/Unseen/words spoken behind the back

Neck
color: _____ shape: _____ word: _____
Authority/power

Head
color: _____ shape: _____ word: _____
Authority

Face
color: _____ shape: _____ word: _____
Heart/presence

Hair
color: _____ shape: _____ word: _____
Covering

SUMMARY: _____

_____

_____

_____

_____

_____

_____

_____

_____

Body Conclusion

_____

_____

_____

_____

_____

_____

_____

_____

Body Representation Chart

BODY PART	REPRESENTS	REFERENCE
FEET	PATH/TYPE OF WALK	Num 20:19
ANKLES	FAITH	Acts 3:7
CALF/SHIN/LEG	RUNNING AFTER/TO	Is. 47:2
KNEE	SUBMISSION	Gen 41:43
THIGH	STRENGTH OF STANCE/ COVENANT	Gen 24:2
HIPS	BALANCE	Gen. 32:24,30
GROIN	REPRODUCTION, NEEDS COVERING, WHAT WE PRODUCE, READY FOR SERVICE, SEAT OF STRENGTH/VIGOR	Job 31:20, Gen. 35:11 Ex. 12:11, Job 40:16
BACK	PAST/UNSEEN	Gen 19:26
SHOULDERS	WEIGHT CARRIED	Gen 21:14
STOMACH/BELLY	CORE OF BEING/ REPRODUCTION	1Kings 7:20
CHEST/BREAST	HEART/WHAT BEING NURTURED/INTELLECT	Job 24:9, Gen. 6:5
NECK	AUTHORITY/POWER	Deut 28:48
FACE	HEART (FEELINGS SHOWING ON FACE) PRESENCE	Ex 10:28
HEAD	AUTHORITY	Gen 3:15
HAIR	COVERING	Num 6:5
ARM	STRENGTH	Ex 6:6
HAND/WRIST	POWER/DOMINION	Gen 3:23

Color Chart

COLOR	GOOD REFERENCE	NEGATIVE REFERENCE
Black	Deep things of God (Gen 49:25) God's judgment (Rev 6:5)	Lack, Sin, Demonic, Bondage (Lam 5:10)
Blue - Dark (Hyacinth)	Holy service (Ex 28:31) Chastening (Pr 20:30) Healing (Matt 12:20-21)	Bruised, Danger, Attack (Rev 9:17)
Blue - Light (Violet)	Holy Spirit, Sacred (Ex 25:4) Gate, Covering (Ex 27:16) heavenly (Ex 24:10)	Worldly, Whoredoms, Spiritual Adultery (Jer 10:8-9)
Brown	Singled out, Marked (Gen 30:32)	Dead, Like dry grass (1Peter 1:24)
Gold (betser, charats)	Pure, Holy (Job 22:24, Ps 68:13, Lam 4:2, Matt 2:11, Matt 23:16)	Idol (Is 2:20)
Green	Provision, Peace, New growth (Gen 1:30, Ps 23:2, Ps 52:8)	Jealousy, Envy, Carnal (1Peter 1:24)
Grey	Honor, Wisdom (Lev 19:32, Pr 20:29)	Confusion, Lack of Direction, Sorrow (Gen 42:38)
Orange	Holy Spirit Fire (Acts 2:3)	Danger (fire is orange) (Matt 5:22, Pr 6:27)
Pink (basar-rosy)	Innocent, Fresh (Gen 2:21)	Immature, Capped, Corrupt (Gen 6:12, 2 Kings 5:14)
Purple	Royal, Wealth, Authority (Dan 5:29)	Bruised, Torment (Luke 16:19)
Red	Blood of Jesus, New Covenant (Matt 26:28)	Sin, Anger, Rage, Fire (Is 1:18, Rev 6:4, Rev 9:17)

COLOR	GOOD REFERENCE	NEGATIVE REFERENCE
Silver (Kaceph)	Knowledge, Wealth, Wisdom, Righteousness (Pr 2:1-7, Ps 68:13, Pr 25:2-5)	Idol, Betrayal (Is 2:20, Matt 27:3-10)
White	Pure (Rev 19:8)	Imposter (2Cor 11:14)
Yellow	Gift, Covering, God-like (Ps 68:13, Rev 9:17)	Disease, Fear (Yellow-belly) (Lev 13:30)

Color Combination Chart

COLOR COMBINATION	REFERENCE	MEANING
Orange & Black	(Halloween Colors)	Witchcraft, Extreme danger
Purple & Dark Blue Today's meaning of black & blue	Royal Covering Bruised Spirit	
Purple & Gold	Traditional colors of Royalty	Royal, Gifting, Pure
Rainbow Colors	Rev 4:3 Gen 9:13 (Today's Society)	God's Promise Covenant, Peace Perversion

Shapes

SHAPE	POSITIVE REFERENCE	NEGATIVE REFERENCE
Arch/Bow	Covenant, Peace, Gateway, Entrance, Tabernacle, Authority, Strength (Gen 9:13, Ez 40)	Stubborn, Cruel H7185* *Strong's Concordance
Circle or Dot	Presence of the Lord. i.e., His sitting place, His path in heaven and in Creation. To be surrounded, Grace, Family, Unending love "To come full circle" (Is 40:22, Job 22:14, Pr 8:27)	Running in circles* * Today's vernacular
Hexagon	God's chosen (Jews) Star of David	Idolatrous worship, Witchcraft, Magic, Abortion, Murder (Moloc), Fertility, Sex, War (Astarte)
Oblong	Door-like, Opening, Faith, Protection, Shield, Covering (Eph 6:16)	Spiritual Warfare H2375* *Strong's Concordance
Octagon	Salvation, Rebirth, Cutting away of old, Regeneration, Covenant, Resurrection	Stop *Today's vernacular
Oval	Birthed or about to birthed, Grace stretched (Deut 22:6)	Loss of flavor (Job 6:6)

SHAPE	POSITIVE REFERENCE	NEGATIVE REFERENCE
Square	Repentance, Dwelling with the Lord, Inheritance (1Kings &:5, Ez 43:16, Ez 45:2)	Judgment, Boxed in,* Set boundaries (1Kings 7:5) * Today's vernacular
Star	A star (round or shining). A prince Gen. 1:16	To prick, penetrate, blister, eating into, burn Gen. 1:16 Strongs H3554
Straight	Pleasant, Prosperous, Well done, Study, Discernment, Truth, Path, To stand Straight-laced (1Sam 6:12, 2Tim 2:15)	Obstacles, Rigid, 'Immovable/Stubborn' Matt 7:14
Triangle	Door, Trinity, 3 cord braid, Hierarchy, Authority (Gen 18:1)	Bad outside influences Can speak of polluted doors "Today's vernacular"

Directions

DIRECTION	POSITIVE REFERENCE	NEGATIVE REFERENCE
Down	Subdue, Conquer, Take down (Gen 11:5)	Descend, Boundary, Enemy, Fall, Hades (Matt 8:1)
East	Rise up, New beginning, Goal, Prophetic (Gen 2:14, Matt 2:1)	Hurry, Prevent, Intense, Repeat (Gen 2:14, Matt 2:1)

Horizontal	Agape love, Spiritual manifestations (Gal 5:22-25) Worship, Supplication* *extreme prayer posture	Carnal manifestations (Gal 5:19-21) Knocked down* * Today's vernacular
Left (see north)	Spiritual, Mantle, Resemble, Take away sin (Gen 13:9)	Dark, Idol, Second-best H5566* *Strong's Concordance
North	Protect, Secret place, Wind, Holy Spirit (Luke 13:29)	Hidden, Dark, Unknown (Gen 28:14)
Right (see south)	Physical, Strength, Favor, Authority, Sanctified (Gen 13:9)	Parched, Desert, Bondage (Gen 12:9)
South (see down)	Joining, Together, Gentle (Acts 8:26)	Parched, Desert, Bondage (Gen 12:9)
Up	Ascend, Increase, Restore, Work, Launch, Lead (Gen 2:6, Matt 4:1)	Burn, Cut off (Gen 2:6)
Vertical	Rebuild, Measure, recalibrate, Agape love (Amos 7:7-9, Zec 4)	Judgment (Amos 7:7-9)
West (see down)	Roar, Rise up, Pound (Gen 12:8)	End, Sink, Go down (Matt 8:11)

Stones

NAME	DESCRIPTION	MEANING	REF.
Beryl	Topaz colored	Heb rāšaš "Destroy, Crush"	Ex 28:20
Coral	Rose - Pink	Heb Ramwt "to be high"	Job 28:18, Pr 24:7
Crystal	Clear, Glassy	Heb Ghbsh "Glassy Substance" root word "To freeze" "Ice"	Job 28:18, Ez 11:22
Diamond	Hard, Transparent	Heb Shmyr "Diamond" "Hard" "Emery"	Ez 3:9, Jer 17
Jasper	red, yellow, brown, or green, rarely blue	Heb lāban "to show oneself purified"	Ex 28:20
Pearl	White-Blue tones, Sometimes shades of pink or yellow. Other colors do exist	Arabic dar "Pearl" Relates to Wisdom	Job 28:18
Sapphire	Different colors	Heb 'ārar to strip, demolish, lay bare	Song 5:14
Turquoise	Greenish, Blue	"Spring of Gladness" Can mean healing	Ex 28:15-23 Gk5876* Strong's Concordance

Metals

METAL	POSITIVE REFERENCE	NEGATIVE REFERENCE
Brass/Copper	Divine, learn by experience, diligently observe. Dan 2:32 Holy offering that was weighed Ezra 8	spell; enchanter,, diligently observe. Filthiness Dan 2:32
Clay	To be thick or dense 1Kings 7:46 To boil, to bubble up Job 4:19 Dirt being swept away Ps 40:2	To peel, scale or shred Dan 2:33 cunning, secret Lev 6:28 a demon, calamity Ps 40:2
Gold	Shimmer, Fair weather, Pure Dan. 2:32 To be blessed by the Lord. Gen 24:35 Honor Gen 41:42	Idolatry Ex 32:4
Iron	Strength Deut 33:25 Valuable 1Chr 22:14 For Service 1 Chr 29:7	To pierce Dan 2:33 Judgment Lev 26:19 Warfare Judges 4:3 Bondage Ps 149:8 revolt, slander, corruptors Jer 6:28
Lead		Worthless Ez 22:18
Silver	Wealth, Blessings Gen 13:2	Fear, to pine for, to be greedy Dan 2:32 Betrayal, evil covenant Matt 26:15 Idolatry Rev 9:20
Tin	Riches, to select, distinguish Ez 27:12	To separate or divide Num 31:22 Dross, worthless Is. 1:25 Judgment Ez 22:20

Weapons/Items

ITEM	POSITIVE REFERENCE	NEGATIVE REFERENCE
Arrow	Lord's deliverance (2Kings 13:17)	Bitter words (Ps 64:3)
Bronze	Christ's judgment for or against (Rev 1:13,15)	Judgment (Ex 27:2) alter
Circle	God's presence (Is 40:22) What is approaching (Job 22:14) Surround an enemy (Chr 14:14)	To sink into (Ex 35:22) root To sink/drown (Is 3:21)
Copper/Brass	Something traded/Currency (Matt 10:29)	Lacking love (1Cor 13:1) Idol (Rev 9:20)
Gates/Door	Entrance/Christ/Access (John 10:7)	Speech, Mouth (Ps 141:3)
House	The Lord's temple (Matt 21:13) Family Bloodline (Gen 7:1)	Demon Residence (Matt 12:29)
Knife	Revelation (Titus 1:13)	Accusations, Gossip (Ps 52:2)
Metal	To pour out or cast (Job 37:18)	Stronghold, Burden, Sin, Bondage (Deut 28:48)
Rainbow	Peace, Covenant (Gen 9:13)	Perverted Covenant, Homosexual* *Today's vernacular

ITEM	POSITIVE REFERENCE	NEGATIVE REFERENCE
Sticks	Handstaff, Guiding, Divining (1Sam 17:43)* H4731 Strong's Concordance	Strike, Hit (1Sam 17:43)
Sword	Word of God (Eph 6:17)	Sharp words (Pr 12:18)
Tower	The Lord (2 Sam 22:51)	To make large, Pride (Gen 11:4)* H4026 root Strong's Concordance
Walls	Protection (1Sam 25:16)	Barrier, Unbelief (Pr 18:11)

Note: Any item can contain something else within it.

Spirit Location

Spirit	Location	Reference
Anger	Chest//Nose/Forehead/Face	Eccl 7:9/Gen 27:45
Bitterness	Heart/Mouth	Pr 14:10/Rom 3:14
Bondage	Ankles/neck/wrists	Duet. 28:48/Ps 105:18
Broken Spirit	Bones	Pr 17:22
Confusion	Face	Jer 7:19
Curse	Chest	Jer 32:18
Destruction	Feet/Path	Is 59:7
Envy	Bones	Pr 14:39
Error	Feet/Path	Jude 11
Familiar	Face/Mouth	Is 8:19
Fear	Heart/Head	Luke 21:26/2 Tim 1:7
Iniquity	Chest	Job 31:33
Jealousy	Heart/Mind	Song 8:6/2 Cor 11:2
Lethargy	Chest/Eyes	Pr 19:24/Is 29:9
Lying	Tongue/jaw	Is 9:17
Mocking	Mouth	Gal 6:7
Perverse	Feet/Path/Mouth	Is 59:8/Pr 8:13
Pride	Mouth/Neck/Heart/Head/Feet	Ps 59:12/Ps 73:6/Jer 49:16/Is 28:3/Dan 4:37
Python	Hips/rib/respiratory (choking)	(My own experience)
Rebellion	Back/Neck/Feet/Heart	Neh 9:17/Pr 6:18
Reproach/Rejection	Chest	Ps 89:50
Slanderer	Foot	Gen 8:9
Stubbornness	Neck/shoulders/heart	2Kings 17:14/2Chr 36:13/Neh 9:17

GLOSSARY

Astral Projection—sending astral body out (*Bing Dictionary*)

Automatic Writing—involuntary or unconscious writing (*Bing Dictionary*)

Body Lifting—the ability to lift a body with fingers

Clairvoyance—seeing what is not normally seen (*Bing Dictionary*)

Crystal Ball——a fortuneteller's globe: a clear solid sphere of glass or rock crystal that is used by a fortuneteller for supposedly predicting the future (*Bing Dictionary*)

Curse——an evil prayer: a malevolent appeal to a supernatural being for harm to come to somebody or something, or the harm that is thought to result from this (*Bing Dictionary*)

Dowsing——using a divining rod: to use a divining rod to search for underground water or minerals (*Bing Dictionary*)

ESP—parapsychology: extrasensory perception (*Bing Dictionary*)

Fortune-Teller—somebody who claims to foretell

the future: somebody who predicts the future, e.g. by divination

Horoscope——an astrological forecast: an astrologer's description of the personality and future of a person based on the position of the planets in relation to the sign of the zodiac under which the person was born (*Bing Dictionary*)

Hypnosis——an artificially induced condition: a condition that can be artificially induced in people, in which they can respond to questions and are very susceptible to suggestions from the hypnotist (*Bing Dictionary*)

Levitation—to rise into the air: to rise and float in the air, or make something rise and float in the air, seemingly in defiance of gravity (*Bing Dictionary*)

Magic—supposed supernatural power: a supposed supernatural power that makes impossible things happen or gives somebody control over the forces of nature. (*Bing Dictionary*)

Mediums— a person claiming to be in contact with the spirits of the dead and to communicate between the dead and the living. (*Webster's Dictionary*)

Metaphysics—the branch of philosophy that deals with the first principles of things, including abstract concepts such as being, knowing, substance, cause, identity, time, and space.(*Webster's Dictionary*)

Mind Reading—the ability to sense others' thoughts.

Palm Reading—a person who is supposedly able to predict someone's future by interpreting the lines on the palms of their hands (*Webster's Dictionary*)

Psychometry—divination by touching an object: the alleged ability to obtain information about a person or event by touching an object related to that person or event (*Bing Dictionary*)

Reincarnation—being reborn into another body: in some systems of belief, a person or animal in whose body somebody's soul is born again after he, she, or it has died (*Bing Dictionary*)

Séance—a meeting whose purpose is to speak with dead: a meeting at which a spiritualist attempts to receive communications from the spirits of the dead

Second Sight—the supposed ability to perceive future or distant events; clairvoyance. (*Webster's Dictionary*)

Spirit of Divination—-the practice of using signs (such as an arrangement of tea leaves or cards) or special powers to predict the future (*Merriam Webster's Dictionary*)

Table Tipping—a type of séance in which participants sit around a table, place their hands on it, and wait for rotations. The table was purportedly made to serve as a means of communicating with the spirits; the alphabet would be slowly called over and the table would tilt at the appropriate letter, thus spelling out words and sentences. The process is similar to that undertaken with a Ouija board. (*Wikipedia*)

Tarot—fortune-telling with cards: a system of fortune-telling using a special pack of 78 cards consisting of 4 suits of 14 cards together with 22 picture cards (*Bing Dictionary*)

Tea Leaf Reading——a divination or fortune-telling method that interprets patterns in tea leaves, coffee grounds, or wine sediments (*Wikipedia*)

Water Witching—discovering of subterranean streams by means of a divining rod

Witchcraft——the alleged effect of magical powers: the alleged effect or influence of magical powers (*Bing Dictionary*)

Yoga—a Hindu spiritual and ascetic discipline, a part of which, including breath control, simple meditation, and the adoption of specific bodily postures, is widely practiced for health and relaxation. The yoga widely known in the West is based on hatha yoga, which forms one aspect of the ancient Hindu system of religious and ascetic observance and meditation, the highest form of which is raja yoga and the ultimate aim of which is spiritual purification and self-understanding leading to *samadhi* or union with the divine. (*Webster's Dictionary*)

END NOTES

1   *Strong's Hebrew and Chaldee Dictionary of the Old Testament*, Oak Tree Software, version 2.9. H342
2   Ibid., H2233
3   Ibid., H7779
4   Ibid., H7218
5   Ibid., H6119
6   *Strong's Greek Dictionary of the New Testament*, Oak Tree Software, version 2.6, Gk372
7   Ibid., Gk3624
8   Ibid., Gk4980
9   Ibid., Gk4563
10   Ibid., Gk2885
11   "Can born-again believers be demon possessed?" (1972, May). In *ag.org*. Retrieved January 5, 2016.
12   Prince, D. (1998). *They Shall Expel Demons* (p. 143). Ada, MI: Chosen Books.
13   Prince, D. (1998). *They Shall Expel Demons* (p. 16). Ada, MI: Chosen Books.
14   Ibid., Gk3180
15   Ibid., Gk2078 root word Gk 1510
16   Ibid., Gk756
17   Ibid., Gk1849
18   Ibid., Gk2888 and Gk4655
19   Ibid., Gk4189 and Gk2032
20   Ibid., Gk1849
21   Ibid., Gk3961 root word Gk3817
22   Ibid., Gk3789 root word Gk3700

23 Ibid., Gk4651 root word Gk4649

24 Ibid., Gk1411

25 Kazenske, Donna J., Spiritual Orphans,. retrieved from http://purewordministries.net/spiritualorphans,

26 *Strong's Greek Dictionary of the New Testament*, Oak Tree Software, version 2.6, Gk1980 compound root word Gk1909 and Gk4649

27 Ibid., H1281

28 Ibid., H6129

29 Ibid., Gk2375

30 Newitz, Annalee, April 2, 2009, *Batteries that Feed on Blood*, retrieved from io9.com

31 *Strong's Hebrew and Chaldee Dictionary of the Old Testament*, Oak Tree Software, version 2.9 H4832

32 Ibid., H5558

33 Ibid., H7667

34 Ibid., H2580

35 Wright, Henry, 2009, *A More Excellent Way*, Kensington, PA, Whitaker House, pg 65

36 Nelson's Illustrated Bible Dictionary, Thomas Nelson Publishers, Copyright © 1986,

37 Jamieson, Fausset, and Brown Commentary, Electronic Database. by Biblesoft, Inc. Copyright © 1997, 2003

38 *Strong's Hebrew and Chaldee Dictionary of the Old Testament*, Oak Tree Software, version 2.9, H990

39 Ibid., H6529

40 Ibid., H3027

41 Ibid., H157

42 Ibid., H398

43 Ibid., H6529

44 *Strong's Greek Dictionary of the New Testament*, Oak Tree Software, version 2.6, Gk1210

45 Ibid., Gk 3089

46 Ibid., Gk 3772

47 Norvell, Scott J,. 2007-2010, *Terraforming for the Kingdom*, page 26

48 *Strong's Greek Dictionary of the New Testament*, Oak Tree Software, version 2.6, Gk1656

49 Kruglinski, Susan, (April 2009). *The Man Who Found Quarks and Made Sense of the Universe.* Discover Magazine

50 DragonlordALS, (June 13, 2004). *String Theory.* Retrieved from urbandictionary.com/define.php?term=string

51 Holloway, April, (December 3, 2013). *Researchers reveal Stonehenge hold incredible musical properties.* Retrieved from www.ancientorigins. net/news-history-archaeology/*Researchers reveal Stonehenge hold incredible musical properties,*

52 *Secret Power Sounds Decoded (webpage)*

53 *Secret Power Sounds Decoded (webpage)*

54 University of Pennsylvania Perelman School of Medicine, October 30, 2006, *Language Center of the Brain Is Not Under the Control of Subjects Who "Speak in Tongues"*

55 Burns, Phyllis Doyle, May 12, 2015, Australian Aboriginal Dreamtime - Sacred Era of Creation. Retrieved from http://phyllisdoyle.hubpages. com/hub/Australian-Aboriginal-Dreamtime-Sacred-Era-of-Creation

56 Milligan, Ira, 199, *Understanding the Dreams you Dream*, Shippensburg, PA, 1st ed., pg 8

57 Ibid., pp. 23, 27

58 Ibid., p. 25

59 Amplified Bible, Oak Tree Software, version 2.6

60 Ibid.

61 *Strong's Greek Dictionary of the New Testament*, Oak Tree Software, version 2.6, Gk 3772

Printed in the United States
By Bookmasters